Job Rights & Survival Strategies

A HANDBOOK FOR TERMINATED EMPLOYEES

NATIONAL
EMPLOYEE
RIGHTS
INSTITUTE
(NERI)

HELPING
EMPLOYEES
UNDERSTAND,
ENFORCE,
AND EXPAND
THEIR RIGHTS
IN THE
WORKPLACE

BY ATTORNEYS PAUL H. TOBIAS AND SUSAN SAUTER

1997

❖ DEDICATION

*This book is dedicated to the
working men and women of America.*

Job Rights & Survival Strategies Copyright © 1997 ISBN 0-9656000-0-9
Published by National Employee Rights Institute (NERI), Cincinnati,
Ohio. All rights reserved. Printed in the United States of America.

Disclaimer
This book provides information on laws governing the workplace. It
should in no way be construed as giving legal advice about the legality of
any particular termination or conduct of an employer. The text does not
purport to list every provision or interpretation of the laws described.
This book should be used as a guide only. If at any time you have questions about whether or how certain laws apply to you specifically, seek the
advice of an attorney.

01 00 99 98   5 4 3 2

Library of Congress Cataloging in Publication Data

Tobias, Paul H., 1930-
    Job rights & survival strategies : a handbook for terminated employees
/ by Paul H. Tobias & Susan Sauter for the National Employee Rights Institute.
        p.   cm.
    ISBN 0-9656000-0-9 (pbk.)
    1. Employees–Dismissal of–Law and legislation–United States.
2. Displaced works–United States–Handbooks, manuals, etc.
I. Sauter, Susan, 1955- . II. National Employee Rights Institute.
III. Title.
KF3471.Z9T63 1997   97-4319
344.7301'2596–dc21   CIP

Cover & text designed by Pam Koenig.

About NERI

The National Employee Rights Institute (NERI) is a nonprofit membership organization founded in 1993 with one purpose: to help employees understand, enforce, and expand their rights in the workplace. This mission is accomplished through a variety of education, advocacy, and research activities.

EDUCATION NERI is the co-publisher, with Chicago-Kent College of Law, of the *Employee Rights and Employment Policy Journal*, a semi-annual publication featuring articles on employment law related issues (Volume 1, Number 1 appeared in March 1998). NERI is also the sponsor of the Employee Rights Clearinghouse which provides information and assistance by way of publications, telephone, and the Internet.

ADVOCACY NERI tracks federal, state, and local legislation and case law related to employee rights and engages in public interest litigation and public policy advocacy. NERI's Chet Levitt Fund provides expenses in public interest cases.

RESEARCH NERI is convening an "Employee Rights Think Tank" to engage in research, education, public and media relations, and policy development in order to influence public opinion concerning employment issues.

NERI experts are available to speak at conferences and seminars on various aspects of employee rights, including such topics as federal discrimination law, right to privacy, and challenging unlawful termination.

In addition, NERI has established the National Employees Organization (NEO) to provide individual employees, especially those who have no other representation, a forum for the exchange of ideas and information as well as benefits and services.

For information about membership and activities, contact NERI at 414 Walnut Street, Suite 911, Cincinnati, Ohio 45202. NERI can also be reached via telephone, 1-800-469-NERI (6374), fax (513) 241-7863, e-mail, mail@nerinet.org, or website: http:\\www.nerinet.org. Contributions in support of NERI's work are tax deductible.

About the Authors

Paul H. Tobias is the senior partner in the firm of Tobias Kraus & Torchia in Cincinnati, Ohio. He is the author of numerous articles in the field of labor and employment law, and a three-volume work, *Litigating Wrongful Discharge Claims* (Callaghan Company, 1987). Mr. Tobias is a graduate of Harvard College (A.B. 1951) and Harvard Law School (LL.B. 1958). He is the co-founder and chairman of the National Employee Rights Institute (NERI) and founder of the National Employment Lawyers Association (NELA).

Susan Sauter earned her law degree at the University of Cincinnati College of Law (J.D. 1991). After working as a staff attorney for the U.S. Department of Labor, Office of Administrative Law Judges, she entered the private practice of law specializing in employment cases. Ms. Sauter graduated summa cum laude from Ohio State University (B.A. 1988) with a degree in English. Currently, she is a law clerk with the Ohio Court of Appeals, 1st District.

ACKNOWLEDGEMENTS

NERI would like to recognize and thank the numerous individuals and organizations who contributed their time, expertise, and wisdom to the production of this handbook. If it is both comprehensive and comprehensible, it is because of them.

Kristine Barr,
Cincinnati, Ohio

Susan Bozorth,
Cincinnati, Ohio

Dina Brock,
Union, Kentucky

Jean Busmeyer,
Cincinnati, Ohio

David Cashdan,
Washington, D.C.

John Chevedden,
Redondo Beach, California

Sharon Dietrich,
Philadelphia, Pennsylvania

Mark Dressler,
Traverse City, Michigan

Debra Evans,
Cincinnati, Ohio

Vicki Golden,
Washington, D.C.

Steve Goodman,
Cincinnati, Ohio

H. Candace Gorman,
Chicago, Illinois

David Holdsworth,
Salt Lake City, Utah

Michael Hoover,
Cincinnati, Ohio

Don Hurst,
Cincinnati, Ohio

Richard Johnson,
Tallahassee, Florida

Penny Nathan Kahan,
Chicago, Illinois

Joseph Kaplan,
Washington, D.C.

Jonathan Kroner,
Miami Beach, Florida

Robert L. Liebross,
Denver, Colorado

Patricia Losacker,
Loveland, Ohio

Lewis Maltby,
New York, New York

Wayne Outten,
New York, New York

Donald Petersen,
Orlando, Florida

Ann Ramsey,
Cincinnati, Ohio

Richard Rosenthal,
Cincinnati, Ohio

Douglas Scherer,
Huntington, New York

Jim Sitlington,
Cincinnati, Ohio

Vlad Spitzer,
Stamford, Connecticut

Emily Stout,
Cincinnati, Ohio

Eliza Tobias,
Cincinnati, Ohio

David Torchia,
Cincinnati, Ohio

Robert White,
Cincinnati, Ohio

We are particularly grateful to our editor, Monique Rothschild, of Cincinnati, Ohio, who directed several revisions, made valuable suggestions about the content, and refined our prose.

CONTENTS

13 INTRODUCTION   **PROLOGUE: CAN THIS JOB BE SAVED?**   **15**

Keep Your Cool   15
Explore Your Options   16
File Your Appeal   16

19 PART I: FIRST THINGS FIRST— GETTING OUT THE DOOR

CHAPTER ONE: ENDING THE EMPLOYMENT RELATIONSHIP   **20**

PERSONAL AND PERSONNEL FILES   20
VERIFY THE REASON FOR YOUR TERMINATION   21
CONSIDER RESIGNING   21
GET LETTERS OF REFERENCE   23
THINK TWICE BEFORE SIGNING ANYTHING   24
Releases   24
Non-Compete Clauses and Restrictive Covenants   25
Confidentiality Requirements   26
DON'T BURN YOUR BRIDGES   27
KEEP A RECORD OF EVENTS   28

29 PART II: TAKING CARE OF YOUR FINANCES

CHAPTER TWO: SEPARATION PACKAGE CONSIDERATIONS   **30**

SEVERANCE PAY   30
VACATION AND SICK PAY   32
RETIREMENT AND SAVINGS PLANS   32
Defined Benefit Plans   32
Defined Contribution Plans   33
Early Retirement   33
Vesting   33
Regulation of Pensions   34
How Termination Affects Your Plan   34
Savings Plans   34
Withdrawal of Funds at Termination   34
STOCK OPTIONS   35
MAKE SURE YOU WERE PROPERLY PAID   36

CHAPTER THREE: NEGOTIATING YOUR OWN SEPARATION PACKAGE   **37**

WHO HAS THE AUTHORITY TO NEGOTIATE?   38
HOW TO NEGOTIATE   38
INCREASE YOUR BARGAINING POWER   40
STRESS YOUR STRENGTHS   41
HOW MUCH CAN YOU EXPECT TO GET?   41

GET CREATIVE	**42**
Redefine the Termination	42
Become a Consultant	43
Defer the Effective Date of Termination	43
Convert Unneeded Benefits to Cash	43

CHAPTER FOUR: UNEMPLOYMENT COMPENSATION: YOU ARE ENTITLED, OR ARE YOU? — **45**

WHY WERE YOU TERMINATED?	**45**
WHAT IF YOUR EMPLOYER CONTESTS?	**46**
DID YOU QUIT?	**47**
DID YOU RECEIVE SEVERANCE PAY?	**48**
ARE YOU A UNION EMPLOYEE?	**48**
HOW CAN YOU MAKE THE BEST OF THE SYSTEM?	**48**
PROVIDING INFORMATION	**50**

CHAPTER FIVE: PUBLIC ASSISTANCE — **51**

CHAPTER SIX: HEALTH INSURANCE — **52**

CONTINUATION OF COVERAGE	**52**
NOTIFICATION	**52**
PREMIUM PAYMENT	**53**
GROSS MISCONDUCT	**53**
FAMILY COVERAGE	**53**
PORTABILITY	**54**

55 PART III: TERMS OF EMPLOYMENT

CHAPTER SEVEN: WHAT RULES PROTECT YOU IF... — **56**

...YOU ARE A PRIVATE SECTOR EMPLOYEE	**56**
...YOU ARE A UNION EMPLOYEE	**57**
...YOU ARE A GOVERNMENT EMPLOYEE	**58**
...YOU ARE AN INDEPENDENT CONTRACTOR	**59**
...YOU WORK FOR A TEMPORARY EMPLOYMENT AGENCY	**60**

CHAPTER EIGHT: CONTRACTS AND PROMISES — **61**

WHAT IS A CONTRACT?	**61**
Written Contracts	62
Oral Contracts	63
Implied Contracts	63
What is an Enforceable Promise?	63
The Covenant of Good Faith and Fair Dealing	64

65 **PART IV:** | **CHAPTER NINE:**
A CRASH | **FEDERAL LAWS THAT PROTECT WORKERS** 66
COURSE IN
EMPLOYMENT | **THE NATIONAL LABOR RELATIONS ACT** 66
LAW | **THE CIVIL RIGHTS ACT OF 1964** 67
Race, Color, National Origin or Sex Discrimination 67
Religious Discrimination 69
THE AGE DISCRIMINATION IN EMPLOYMENT ACT 69
THE AMERICANS WITH DISABILITIES ACT 70
Anti-Discrimination 70
Reasonable Accommodation 71
THE FAMILY AND MEDICAL LEAVE ACT 72
THE "ANTI-RETALIATION" PROVISIONS OF
THE FEDERAL STATUTES 73
THE WORKER ADJUSTMENT RETRAINING AND
NOTIFICATION ACT 73
THE EMPLOYEE POLYGRAPH PROTECTION ACT 74
THE EMPLOYEE RETIREMENT INCOME AND
SECURITY ACT 75
THE RAILWAY LABOR ACT 76
THE RACKETEER INFLUENCED AND
CORRUPT ORGANIZATIONS ACT 76
THE UNIFORMED SERVICES EMPLOYMENT AND
REEMPLOYMENT RIGHTS ACT OF 1994 76
THE CONSUMER CREDIT PROTECTION ACT 76
THE JUROR PROTECTION ACT 76
OTHER CIVIL RIGHTS ACTS 77
THE FALSE CLAIMS ACT 77
THE IMMIGRATION AND NATURALIZATION ACT 78
FEDERAL ANTI-TRUST LAWS 78
THE BANKRUPTCY ACT 78
THE WHISTLEBLOWER PROTECTION ACT 78
THE FEDERAL CIVIL SERVICE REFORM ACT 79
THE EQUAL PAY ACT 79
THE FAIR LABOR STANDARDS ACT 80

CHAPTER TEN: STATE LAW PROTECTION 82

UNLAWFUL DISMISSALS 82
OTHER UNLAWFUL CONDUCT—TORTS 82
Intentional Infliction of Emotional Distress 83
Defamation 83
Invasion of Privacy 84
Fraud 85
Assault and Battery 85
False Imprisonment 86
Violation of Public Policy 87
Negligence 88
Interference in the Employment Relationship 88

CHAPTER ELEVEN:
WERE YOU DISCRIMINATED AGAINST? 89

    DISCRIMINATION CLAIMS 89
    Evidence of Discrimination 89
    Countering Your Employer's Denials 91
    RETALIATION CLAIMS 92
    What is Protected Conduct? 92
    Did Your Employer Take Adverse Action? 93
    Did Your Employer Know About Your Protected Conduct? 93
    Evidence That Your Protected Conduct Led To Your Termination 93
    Countering Your Employer's Denials 94
    ERISA CLAIMS 94
    PERSONS PROTECTED BY FEDERAL LAW 95

---

97 **PART V:**
    TAKING ACTION

**CHAPTER TWELVE: MAKE SURE TIME
DOESN'T RUN OUT—STATUTES OF LIMITATIONS** 98

    FEDERAL LAWS 98
    STATE LAWS 98
    Discrimination Claims 98
    Tort Claims 99
    Contract Claims 99
    STATUTES OF LIMITATIONS 100

CHAPTER THIRTEEN: BUILD YOUR CASE 102

    GATHER DOCUMENTS 102
    IDENTIFY WITNESSES 103
    Written Statements 103
    "Birds of a Feather" 103

CHAPTER FOURTEEN: SEE AN ATTORNEY 104

    FIND EXPERIENCED LEGAL REPRESENTATION 104
    The Local Bar Association 105
    Attorneys Who Have Represented You in the Past 105
    Personal References 105
    The Yellow Pages 105
    The National Employment Lawyers Association 105
    WORKING WITH AN ATTORNEY 106
    The Initial Consultation 106
    The Contract for Services 107
    Attorneys Fees 107
    What the Legal Agreement Covers 108
    The Written Fee Agreement 108
    The Attorney-Client Relationship 108

CHAPTER FIFTEEN: PURSUE AND EXHAUST ALL ADMINISTRATIVE REMEDIES　110

DISCRIMINATION CLAIMS　110
Equal Employment Opportunity Commission　110
Federal Employees　112
UNION CONTRACT VIOLATIONS　112
UNION ACTIVITIES CLAIMS (NLRB)　113
CLAIMS INVESTIGATED BY THE
　DEPARTMENT OF LABOR (DOL)　113
UNSAFE WORKING CONDITIONS CLAIMS (OSHA)　114
STATE LAW CLAIMS (FEP AGENCIES)　115
OTHER CLAIMS　115

CHAPTER SIXTEEN: GOING TO COURT　116

RISK IN PROCEEDING WITHOUT A LAWYER　116
BASIC STAGES IN THE LEGAL PROCESS　117
Complaint and Answer　117
Discovery　117
Motions to Dismiss　118
Settlement　118
Going to Trial　119
Appeals　119
DAMAGES　119
THE ALTERNATIVE DISPUTE
　RESOLUTION OPTION (ADR)　120

123 PART VI: OTHER SURVIVAL STRATEGIES

CHAPTER SEVENTEEN: FINDING ANOTHER JOB　124

NETWORKING　124
RESUMES AND REFERENCES　125
POUNDING THE PAVEMENT　126
Outplacement Services and Employment Agencies　126
Research the Job Market　126
JOB APPLICATIONS AND INTERVIEWS　127
EDUCATION AND TRAINING　128

CHAPTER EIGHTEEN: COPING WITH JOB LOSS　129

LET YOUR SUPPORT SYSTEM BE SUPPORTIVE　129
STAY ACTIVE　130
ALLOCATE YOUR RESOURCES CAREFULLY　130
KEEP FIT AND HEALTHY　130
STEER CLEAR OF DRUGS AND ALCOHOL　131
REST AND SLEEP　131
JOIN A SUPPORT GROUP　131
KEEP A JOURNAL　132
SEEK PROFESSIONAL COUNSELING　132
MAKE TIME TO HAVE A GOOD TIME　133

EPILOGUE   134

APPENDICES   135

    OFFICIAL CITATIONS TO FEDERAL LAWS   136
    FEDERAL GOVERNMENT OFFICES   137
    NON-GOVERNMENTAL RESOURCES   142
    SAMPLE LETTERS OF APPEAL   145
    SAMPLE REFERENCE LETTERS   148
    SAMPLE EEOC CHARGE FORM   149

INDEX   150

INTRODUCTION

Times have changed. Workers used to stay with one company or industry for life. In some industries, during slack periods, workers might have been laid off, but they had the expectation that they would be called back when business improved. This is no longer true. The workplace is less certain, the concept of job security has eroded, and employers often put maximization of profit before the interests of their employees.

SIZING UP DOWNSIZING

Several million workers have been "downsized" since 1990, and corporate America isn't finished yet! Unlike the layoffs of the past, today's well-paid, mid-level managers are as vulnerable as workers on the assembly line. The threat and/or reality of being unemployed is the worst fear of many adults. Both the threat and the reality have a major impact on one's financial, physical, and emotional well being.

> ➤ **FYI**
>
> *Additional copies of Job Rights & Survival Strategies can be ordered using the form at the back of this book. Bulk rates are available.*

To survive in the 1990s and beyond, workers must have stamina, creativity, planning, and a good grasp of their rights. *Job Rights & Survival Strategies* was written to equip readers with enough information about their legal rights to be their own advocates during this critical time, so they can avoid termination altogether in some cases, take steps for effective damage control in others, and move on with confidence in any event.

UNDERSTANDING YOUR BASIC RIGHTS

After you have caught your breath and vented your fears and anger to close friends and family, you can begin to gather your resources, attempt to make the best of a bad situation, educate yourself about your legal rights, and decide whether you have justification for challenging your termination.

Above all, you should feel free to question your employer about your termination, to try to get your job back, and to get everything to which you are entitled. Don't let your employer intimidate you. If you feel uncomfortable talking to your supervisors or feel you can no longer trust them to tell you what is in your best interests, you have the right to turn to others for an explanation of the impact of your termination on employer-sponsored benefits such as health insurance, pensions, and savings plans. You also have the right to take action when you suspect you have been discriminated against or otherwise treated in an unlawful manner.

Job Rights & Survival Strategies provides a detailed road map for navigating the complex universe of the law and legal appeals. It contains an overview of important federal and state laws that protect employees' rights. It provides guidelines for determining whether these rights have been violated, and explains how to develop strategies to enforce these rights or obtain redress when these rights have been violated. It also takes a look at the different rules which apply to private sector, public sector (federal, state, county, municipal), and union workers, with particular attention to the rights of unrepresented (non-union) employees.

COPING WITH JOB LOSS

While you are fighting back, you must devote some of your energy to moving forward. This handbook also offers practical suggestions to help readers make effective use of their time and energy while they remain out of work. Although the focus of this book is not on finding new employment (there are many fine books devoted to that subject), the authors review some basic strategies for job seekers to consider as part of a comprehensive approach to managing the larger problem of job loss.

TAKING ACTION

❖ Make A Note

We invite readers to contribute ideas and suggestions for NERI's next edition of this handbook.

Whether you decide to negotiate for yourself to keep or recover your job, to consult an attorney to represent you, or to file a claim with a state or local agency on your own, reading *Job Rights & Survival Strategies* will help you understand more about "the system" and put you in a stronger position to help yourself. The authors encourage you to contact the National Employee Rights Institute and other organizations listed in the Appendix for additional guidance and support. They hope that the advice and information contained in this guide will ease this transitional period and enable you to maximize your options.

PROLOGUE: CAN THIS JOB BE SAVED?

Whether you have been laid off, downsized, or fired for cause, you have many important decisions to make within the first few hours and days. If you have been with the company for a long time and/or have a job you really love, your first decision might be to fight to keep your job.

Before you panic or pack up your belongings, think about any scenarios under which it might be possible for you to stay with this employer to accumulate more service time and possibly bridge any time needed to fulfill the requirements of your pension or other retirement plan. At the very least, continued employment–no matter how brief–can provide some continuity and income while you are looking for another job.

The first thing to do is get a handle on your employer's policies and practices regarding termination. Go to your human resources or personnel department to obtain a copy of the company's handbook or personnel manual, or any other written statements of company policy. If you can't find anything in writing, ask someone in the department to explain the company's unwritten policies or practices for handling employee complaints or concerns.

If your employer has no set policy, or if the appeals or grievance process that exists has provided you with no relief, there are other methods to exhaust before accepting termination. Find out who has the authority to reinstate you. This could be your immediate supervisor, a department head, an ombudsman, or even the president of the company. Go as high up the chain of command as good sense permits if you really want to hold on to your job or find employment elsewhere in the company. You have nothing to lose and may salvage more than you thought you could.

KEEP YOUR COOL

No matter what the outcome of your attempt to save your job, you will be better off if you remain calm and only sound off to your family and friends–far from the work environment. Angry letters or outbursts make it easier for the company to believe they were justified in terminating you in the first place and to refuse to negotiate with you or your lawyer at a later date. No matter the reason for your termination, go out with dignity. You can acquire a reputation as a problem employee from one emotion-driven tirade. Keep your head, and you can keep your pride as you close this chapter in your working life.

The name of the game at this stage is strategy. You want to win this war and not just the first battle. Therefore, you must consider what is likely to hurt your chances and what is likely to help. If there is a particular supervisor you are sure is on your side, or someone else in top management who is friendly and aware of your good record, you could request a private meeting to explain what you want to do to keep your job and why the company needs you on its team.

EXPLORE YOUR OPTIONS

Once you get the ear of the individual with the authority to rehire you, be prepared to be flexible as well as confident. While your ultimate goal is to get back your job, that may not be a realistic expectation. Make clear your willingness to consider part-time work, contract work, a transfer to another location or subsidiary, or retraining for another position.

Changing the area or division within the company could be especially helpful if the termination was caused by difficulties seeing eye-to-eye with a supervisor or manager. Or, if you suspect that one of the reasons the company let you go was the size of your salary, you could try offering to accept a different pay package, for example one with a lower salary and a performance-based bonus. If your company cites poor performance as the reason for your termination, try asking to return to work on a probationary basis to establish your ability to meet the job requirements.

FILE YOUR APPEAL

If informal efforts to save your job are not successful, you may need to take more formal steps within the company. You must follow the official grievance or complaint process to the letter in challenging your termination. This is true whether it is set out in a handbook or manual or has been explained by company personnel. Ordinarily, such internal appeals or grievance procedures require you to act within a certain amount of time and to communicate with only specified company officials. At each step in the process, you should make a written request for reinstatement to your position and document the company's responses to your arguments. Be persistent but professional. You must exhaust the company's internal grievance procedures before you do anything else to try to get your job back.

Union employees clearly have an advantage when it comes to appealing an unfair or illegal termination. They have detailed grievance procedures to follow. They have designated representatives to negotiate with the employer and present their case for arbitration if necessary. Most non-union employees have to figure out for themselves what steps will be most likely to produce a desired outcome. If their immediate supervisor was the problem, how far up the ladder should they go to lodge a complaint? And if they appear to be doing an "end run" to a higher level manager or administrator, will they be doing themselves more harm than good?

If you want to save your job, you must take whatever steps are appropriate to initiate an appeal at the earliest possible moment—when you first learn that you will probably lose your job or as soon as you receive official notification.

PART I

GETTING OUT THE DOOR

Take a cautious approach to everything that you and your employer say and do about the termination. Anything your employer puts in writing about your termination and the documents you sign before leaving can have important implications for your future. If it's important enough to be in writing, it's important enough to examine with a fine tooth comb. Ask questions and seek an outside opinion if you don't fully understand the answers before you agree to or sign anything.

You will probably see a lot of papers before your last exit. Some, like a summary of your retirement plan status, are fairly routine. However, if you are asked to sign any type of document, take your time. Read the document thoroughly to make sure you understand what you are signing.

Before you take your final leave be sure to obtain letters of reference, make certain you understand the reason for your termination, negotiate the best severance package possible, and make use of all outplacement services available.

At this stage your goals are twofold: to avoid burning bridges and to keep lines of communication open while you still have one foot in the door!

Chapter One

Ending the Employment Relationship

QuickCheck

Documents

✓ Contracts and other proof of hiring or conditions of employment

✓ Notification of promotions and raises

✓ Awards and certificates

✓ Notification of termination

✓ Personnel manual

✓ Benefits contracts

✓ Copies of records in personnel file (if permitted)

Personal and Personnel Files

Make sure you have all documents regarding your employment–hiring and firing, pension and insurance benefits, employer-sponsored savings plans, and any other records relating to your tenure with the company such as training program certificates, evaluations, awards, and letters of commendation. Some of the latter can be put to good use when you apply for a new job. Some documents may also be used in support of a claim if you decide to protest your termination.

If you think you have a good case against your employer, make a list of all documents that may help prove your case. Never take documents or papers that don't belong to you. Never even attempt to access information, either on computer or in company files, that you have no right to know. Anything that is personal to you, such as letters of praise or thanks that were sent to you, can be removed. However, anything related to the company or the operation of the company and its business should not be taken without permission.

While it may be tempting to take confidential company records or access computer files without authorization, this is a big mistake for a number of reasons. First of all, it may be illegal and you might end up facing criminal charges or civil claims as well as trying to fight your termination. Second, it may give the company an excuse to fire you where none existed before. Even if you can prove that you were illegally fired, your employer can use your misconduct to severely limit your ability to recover money or obtain re-employment in a lawsuit. Finally, if you signed a so-called "confidentiality agreement" at the time you were hired, taking confidential documents could subject you to civil action for breach of contract.

An employee's personnel files, including hiring or firing information, salary information, letters to clients, and internal memoranda are the property of the company. You do not have the right to take them with you when you go. Except in

Alaska, California, Connecticut, Delaware, Illinois, Iowa, Maine, Massachusetts, Michigan, Minnesota, Nevada, New Hampshire, New Jersey, Oregon, Pennsylvania, Rhode Island, Washington and Wisconsin, you do not have the legal right to look at the information in your file. Your employer may have a policy allowing access or may honor a request to review the file. Be persistent in your request to copy your file, but realize that your employer may be under no legal obligation to allow you to do so.

VERIFY THE REASON FOR YOUR TERMINATION

If you were fired, attempt to obtain a written statement of the reason(s) for your termination. In some states, your employer is required to give you, upon request, a statement in writing of the reason for your termination. This statement is called a "service letter." States currently requiring such a letter are: California, Maine, Minnesota, Missouri, Montana, Nebraska, Nevada, Oklahoma, Texas, and Washington.

If you cannot obtain a statement in writing, ask your supervisor or manager to tell you the reason. Then write down for yourself the stated reason and include the date, time, and place (and any witnesses) that the statement was given. Read it to the supervisor and make a note of the date he or she confirmed its content.

CONSIDER RESIGNING

When the end of your career with a company seems imminent, or if your working environment has become unbearable, you may be tempted to simply terminate the employment relationship voluntarily by tendering a resignation. Sometimes, a resignation can be helpful. When you apply for new jobs, you can honestly say that you quit the company voluntarily. Your employment record at your old company should reflect that you quit and not that you were fired. For some large companies with numerous affiliates or divisions, an employee who resigns from the job is eligible for rehire with the company at a later date, whereas an employee terminated for cause would not be.

❖ Make A Note

If you come to the conclusion that resignation is your only choice because of severe discrimination, harassment, or other intolerable working conditions, you should indicate in the resignation letter that you are leaving because of these conditions, especially if you plan to take legal action. If you don't, the employer could argue later that if you had really left because of those reasons, you would have said so in your letter.

> **FYI**

You must obtain and read all company documents relating to all of the financial issues discussed before you make the offer to resign, and you are strongly encouraged to consult an attorney.

> **FYI**

If you voluntarily resign, you will not be entitled to unemployment benefits unless you can prove that you were constructively discharged. The availability of company severance pay, the ability to exercise stock options, and the possibility of returning to work for your company at a later date, among other things, can all be affected by a letter of resignation.

However, the difference between being fired or discharged and voluntarily quitting is significant in a number of ways. Whether to resign or be fired is a matter of strategy and depends on the facts of your situation. Before you resign, consult an attorney if you can. An attorney will be able to give you specific information about how a resignation will affect your position. The information below gives some of the general reasons that resignation can be either helpful or hurtful, depending on the circumstances.

It may be that your employer wants to fire you and is making life at work difficult for you, hoping you will quit. The company may refrain from terminating you out of fear that the dismissal would be illegal. Under these circumstances, you may be better off not resigning. If you resign voluntarily, you will be unable to claim an illegal discharge. Assume your employer wants you out but doesn't want to take the possibly unlawful step of discharge. You then can increase your bargaining power with your employer by staying and refusing to resign. You can use the company's desire for your departure as leverage for obtaining a generous separation package. In general, you should try to remain at the job as long as you can to increase your bargaining position. Finally, if your company has an internal grievance procedure, you can appeal the wrongful discharge. If you quit you may not have the right of appeal and your chances of regaining your job (if that is your objective) would be greatly diminished.

If your employment situation is unbearable because of illegal discrimination, you should still try to remain on the job as long as possible. Meanwhile, contact the Equal Employment Opportunity Commission (EEOC) *(see Appendix B)*, the federal agency that investigates claims of discrimination. You are protected from retaliation for filing an EEOC charge or contacting an EEOC investigator. Therefore, any plan to fire you may be put aside at least while the investigation is going on, since the employer does not want to appear to have fired you for filing with the EEOC.

Ordinarily, when an employee proves that he or she was discriminated against by a former employer, the employee is entitled to "back pay," the amount that the employee would have earned at the company had he or she not been discriminatorily terminated. However, if you resign your position because of harassment or discrimination, you would not be entitled to recover back pay unless your resignation is considered a "constructive discharge." To prove constructive discharge, you must prove that your employer made your working conditions so unbearable that you had no other choice but to quit in order to resolve the situation. Usually, you have to show that you tried less drastic means to solve the work problems, such as using an internal appeal process or making complaints to people in the chain of command. A constructive discharge is very hard to prove except in cases of truly egregious harassment. Thus, a resignation might seriously affect your ability to recover for an employer's discriminatory behavior.

As stated earlier, resignation is a matter of strategy and depends on the facts of your situation and your needs after you leave the company. You must obtain and read all company documents relating to all of the financial issues discussed before you make the offer to resign, and you are strongly encouraged to consult an attorney. Whether to quit a job when you think you might want to take legal action against your employer is too important an issue to be left to chance.

GET LETTERS OF REFERENCE

Prospective employers usually ask for references. If you ask them not to contact your former employer, you raise a red flag. A company considering hiring you will probably call your boss anyway, since they don't actually need your permission to call. So, before you completely cut your ties with your employer, find out what your company would say about you to prospective employers. Then try discussing what information you do or do not want released.

It is not illegal for an employer to give out truthful information or opinions about your work. Do not assume that your employer is prohibited by law from giving more than "name, rank and serial number."

Write a generic "to whom it may concern" reference letter about yourself and ask your employer or supervisor to sign it or to use part of it in their own letter. *(See Appendix E for a sample letter of reference.)*

Be prepared to push for a good letter and also be prepared to discuss changes in the exact wording of the letter. A positive letter of reference can go a long way toward improving your employment future.

QuickCheck
The Effective Reference Letter

✓ Stick to the facts. Describe your job duties and time on the job.

✓ Highlight your accomplishments and/or important contributions to the company.

✓ Emphasize your good qualities, without going overboard.

✓ Attach copies of past performance evaluations, if possible.

✓ Ask your employer to put the letter on company letterhead. Have it signed by someone in management or human resources.

✓ Try to get your employer's agreement that any information subsequently given out about you will be taken directly from the letter of reference.

Think Twice Before Signing Anything

Releases

Don't sign any "release" of legal rights or final "settlement" of claims until you either consult a lawyer or are certain you understand all its terms. Releases and settlements written by an employer ordinarily contain a lot of terms that protect your employer. They are not written to help or protect you. Remember, these are the people who just let you go. If they want you to sign something, you can be sure that it's for their benefit, not yours.

What is a release? A "release" or "release of claims" is a legal term for a written statement signed by an employee in which the employee gives up all rights he or she may have to challenge his or her termination and/or to sue the company for its past illegal conduct. A release is like an official pardon given to the company for its unlawful behavior. When you sign a release, you give up valuable rights.

While releases and settlements are common when an employer and employee attempt to reach some kind of resolution of their disputes, you should be suspicious of a release or settlement agreement that your employer insists you must sign immediately, without reviewing it or having it reviewed. You will probably need some time to determine if you have a legal claim that you do not want to give up. Don't be afraid to ask for a week or two weeks to consider and review the release and if necessary to contact a lawyer for counsel and advice.

For employees over age 40, a release of claims is especially complicated. The Older Workers' Benefit Protection Act requires an employer to include certain provisions to make a release of age discrimination claims valid. Some important provisions include the right to consider the release for 21 days before you have to sign it, and the right to revoke the agreement within seven days after the date of signing. If your employer requests a release in exchange for special downsizing benefits that are available to a group of terminated employees, certain statistical information must also be furnished to you. You are strongly encouraged to have such a release reviewed by an attorney before signing it.

> ➤ **FYI**
>
> *Signing documents is not just a formality.*

> ➤ **FYI**
>
> *For employees over age 40, a release of claims is especially complicated. The Older Workers' Benefit Protection Act requires an employer to include certain provisions to make a release of age discrimination claims valid.*

You should not release the following:

- Future claims. Only agree to release the company from liability for any claims that exist up to the date the agreement is signed.

- Pension or retirement claims.

- Workers' compensation claims.

- Claims unrelated to your employment with the company or not arising out of your employment with the company.

NON-COMPETE CLAUSES AND RESTRICTIVE COVENANTS

Carefully review any "non-compete" agreement or "restrictive covenant" you may have signed at the time you were hired. If you signed such a document, you probably agreed not to accept employment in the future with a competitor or engage in other business activities that could compete with the company. The agreement would specify the length of time and geographical range of the restrictions.

Non-compete agreements are generally valid, enforceable contracts if they are entered into without coercion and if they were executed either (1) at the time of hiring or (2) after the employee had already been hired and the employer was providing some incentive or giving something else of value–in legal terms, "consideration"–for the employee to sign the agreement. Usually, the consideration provided by the employer in the second situation is a raise in pay, the ability to participate in stock options, or a promotion to which the employee would not otherwise be entitled. In many states, an agreement that an employee signs after beginning employment or at the time of termination is not valid unless, as stated above, the employer provides consideration to the employee to enter into the agreement.

Reasonable restrictions on your ability to work in a business that competes with your former employer are usually lawful. Whether the agreement is deemed reasonable ordinarily depends on the duration of the restriction (one year? two? five?); its geographic limits (are you prohibited just within your city or does the prohibition extend nationwide?); and the activity prohibited (contacting customers, using information or special training obtained through your old employment).

A one- or two-year restriction within a small geographic location is common and will generally be upheld. One that lasts much longer or restricts you nationwide may be unreasonable. Unreasonable restrictions are not lawful and will not be upheld in court. A court can, however, modify the agreement and enforce reasonable restrictions on your ability to compete. If you violate a non-compete agreement, your former employer may go to court seeking an injunction or court order to stop you from working for a competitor and also to seek damages for any lost profits you may have caused.

Don't assume that simply because your agreement seems unreasonable to you that you are free to ignore the agreement completely and accept employment with a competitor. The "reasonableness" of any particular restriction depends on how the court interprets it. Interpretations vary widely from state to state. It is best to seek legal advice to determine whether the restrictions placed on you will hold up in court.

Both you and a new employer may encounter legal problems if you violate such a non-compete agreement. Your new employer may soon be your old employer if you fail to disclose the existence of the non-compete agreement before you are hired. You should tell your new employer about the restrictive covenant and get their agreement to hire you despite the restriction. You may want to consult a lawyer about the validity and reasonableness of your non-compete agreement and the consequences of violating it.

CONFIDENTIALITY REQUIREMENTS

Many release/settlement agreements include a provision which prohibits you from discussing the terms of a special severance package with anyone. Such provisions are common. In most cases you will be prohibited from discussing the terms of your special severance arrangements with your family (spouses excepted), friends, or co-workers. In exchange, the confidentiality agreement should also require the employer to keep confidential the terms of the agreement and the circumstances of your discharge.

Confidentiality requirements in settlement agreements are not the same as the duty of an employee not to disclose his ex-employer's trade secrets and other confidential information. You have a duty under the law to keep and protect your ex-employer's trade secrets and not to use them for your own benefit.

DON'T BURN YOUR BRIDGES

Anger is a natural response when you lose something as important as your livelihood, especially if you feel that your termination was unfair or unlawful. However, giving in to your anger only hurts you and hinders your attempts to regain your job or make progress toward finding a new job. Don't write your employer a letter in which you finally get off your chest all those things you've wanted to tell your supervisor or employer for years about the horrible way the company is run and the rotten way you've been treated. Such letters never help you, and often hurt. They are usually regarded as confirmation that the company's decision to fire you was correct and proper.

Do not write anything that could be considered an admission that you deserved to be fired. Don't accuse others, especially your supervisor or manager, of misconduct or being incompetent. Remember, just about everyone who could actually help you get your job back will be part of management, and they usually stick together. Don't threaten anyone with physical harm or massive litigation. Examples of harmful threats include:

- "I'll get you for this!"

- "You're going to be sorry you messed with me!"

- "I'll sue you for every dime you've got!"

- "You just bought yourself a million dollar lawsuit!"

- "You fire me and I'll go to 60 Minutes and tell them what really goes on around here!"

Threats will get you nowhere and ordinarily will backfire. A threat of physical violence or extortion might even land you in jail. Likewise, don't make critical remarks about the company, your boss, co-workers, or anyone else in the company. Disparaging comments and threats will label you a trouble maker and damage your position.

❖ Make A Note

If you appeal your termination up the chain of command, you will probably be asked, at sometime, to write a statement about why you think your termination is wrong and unfair and why the VP, ombudsman, or president should agree with you. When you write such a letter, stick to the facts and keep the letter short and simple:

"I was told that I am being fired for _____. I believe that I should not be terminated because a)_____; b)_____; and c)_____. I would like to meet with you to discuss this situation."

Don't get carried away. Your letter should be respectful and less than a page long. (See Appendix D for a sample letter).

KEEP A RECORD OF EVENTS

Keeping a record of events that occur in connection with your job loss will assist you in filling out unemployment compensation forms and in pursuing legal action against your former employer, if you decide to do so.

Memories are often inadequate to recall events with accuracy. List the date, time and place of the event and witnesses. If possible, discretely obtain the home address and home telephone numbers of these individuals.

Try to construct a time line and chronology of important incidents. List important conversations - who said what to whom. Pinpoint the dates as closely as possible. Later, when you need to recall dates and events, you will have a fairly reliable source to turn to.

PART II

TAKE CHARGE OF YOUR FINANCES

While some lucky people have sufficient funds in the bank to cover their expenses for several months after losing their jobs, most terminated workers must take quick action to head off a financial crisis.

For starters, go over all the provisions in the company's personnel manual and other documents relating to the terms of your employment and benefits for information relevant to termination. Next, make an appointment with someone in the company's benefits or human resources office to discuss what you have coming to you in terms of continued benefits and compensation.

Find out immediately if you qualify for severance pay and how much. Even a week or two of additional pay will be important at this juncture. Chapter Three explains how to negotiate a separation package if your company does not automatically offer one, or claims you don't qualify, or offers very little money.

Most employees are permitted to continue in their employer's group health insurance plan at their own expense for a limited period of time after termination of their employment. Chapter Six, "Health Insurance," explains what terminated employees must do to ensure their rights in this area. And finally, apply for unemployment compensation and investigate any public assistance programs for which you may be eligible.

Hardly anything is more important at this stage than preserving your ability to meet your financial obligations.

CHAPTER TWO:
Separation Package Considerations

CHAPTER THREE:
Negotiating Your Own Separation Package

CHAPTER FOUR:
Unemployment Compensation: You Are Entitled, Or Are You?

CHAPTER FIVE:
Public Assistance

CHAPTER SIX:
Health Insurance

Chapter Two
Separation Package Considerations

Most companies give terminated employees a letter or other document outlining what they are entitled to upon separation. Other companies require employees to take the initiative to find out their benefits. This chapter discusses some of the ingredients of the separation package.

Severance Pay

Although employers are not required to do so by law, many give severance pay to some or all permanently laid off or terminated employees. Severance pay is usually calculated according to a set formula, based on your length of service. For example, one employee may qualify for an amount equal to one or two weeks of salary while another may qualify for as much as a year's pay.

You can try to negotiate for more severance than the company offers, especially if you have been with the company for many years, have an excellent service record, or have provided unique services such as being a team leader or bringing in large clients to the company. Sometimes employees who have quit their jobs because of intolerable working conditions can also negotiate for more severance pay than would normally have been provided.

Each company is different. Its personnel practices manual may or may not have a written policy on severance. Or its policy may state that severance will be paid on a case by case basis. If you receive severance pay, there are implications— which are discussed in later chapters – for income tax, unemployment compensation, and potential legal action.

Each method of severance payment – salary continuation or lump sum payment – has its good points and its bad points. Either way, most everything you receive in severance or settlement of legal claims is taxable. Because of a new law passed in 1996, any money recovered for employment discrimination or wrongful discharge claims, whether back pay,

❖ Make A Note

Your employer should not require you to sign a release in order to receive severance pay to which you are already entitled under a company policy. However, if the company voluntarily or as a result of negotiation pays you more severance pay than provided by company policy, you will undoubtedly be required to sign a release of claims.

compensatory damages, or punitive damages, is taxable to you as income in the year you receive it. You might consider deferring part of the payment until the next calendar year to avoid being put in a higher tax bracket. Your employer will withhold from the payments whatever amount is due in taxes.

If you have a choice between the methods for payment of severance, give the following points some thought.

LUMP SUM PAYMENT A lump sum payment is a one-time payment in full of the amount of severance pay that you and your employer have agreed to. After receiving the payment, you need have no further contact with your employer. You do not have to worry that your former employer may somehow make a mistake with payments or cease paying altogether. A lump sum payment gives you immediate funds to invest or use, for example, to hire a professional outplacement service or pay bills.

If you receive a lump sum, your other fringe benefits will usually cease as of the date of the payment. You should also take into account how long you think it will take you to find another job. If you accept a lump sum payment representing 10 weeks' pay, for example, you might not have any further income. You will not be able to ask your former employer for more.

SALARY CONTINUATION When an employer agrees to salary continuation, the employee ordinarily remains on the payroll for a specified length of time and receives pay at the end of each pay period as if he or she were still working. During this time, the employee's fringe benefits, e.g. medical insurance, ordinarily will continue. You can ask for continuation for a set number of weeks, or until you find another job. Generally, state laws will not permit unemployment compensation during the period of salary continuance.

Do not confuse salary continuation with periodic payments. Some employers may want to pay out the severance or settlement amount over time, perhaps 25% immediately, 25% six months later, 25% six months after that, and the final payment after six more months. Don't agree to such an arrangement unless you absolutely have to. Salary continuation is a fairly dependable method of payment of a settlement because the payments are regular. Once an employer agrees to salary

> **FYI**
Most everything you receive in severance or settlement of wrongful termination claims is taxable. Exceptions are payments for physical injuries and medical expenses.

continuation, the information is given to payroll personnel, who send the actual checks. The manager or supervisor who authorized the payments has nothing more to do with it.

However, if the employer agrees to pay periodically over a long period of time, there is room for error and oversight. Missed or late payments are not uncommon. Such uncertainty can sabotage your financial planning and lead to unnecessary conflicts.

VACATION AND SICK PAY

Contrary to popular belief, there are very few states with laws giving you the right to "cash in" your unused vacation or sick time when you leave employment. Most companies that do have a policy regarding payment for unused leave, differentiate between employees who leave voluntarily, those who are laid off, and those who are fired for misconduct. If your employer's policy provides for payment of leave, and you are accused of misconduct, you will either have to negotiate with your employer for payment or sue in court for "breach of contract." Unless the amount of unpaid leave is substantial, legal action is probably not worth the investment of time and money.

RETIREMENT AND SAVINGS PLANS

QuickCheck

Pension Documents to Examine

✓ *Summary plan description*

✓ *Individual benefit statement*

If you participated in a retirement plan, a pension plan, a 401(k) plan, a thrift savings plan, a profit-sharing plan, or any other type of deferred compensation plan, it is absolutely critical that you have all of the documents that describe the plan and your participation in the plan, the status of your account, and how your termination affects your participation in these plans. One important document to which you are entitled is the summary plan description. Another is the individual benefit statement which tells if you are vested and lists your accrued benefits–the amount of your pension at age 65. Study all plan documents thoroughly. Talk to human resources personnel. But you should not rely on oral promises. If there is any doubt concerning your rights, write to the plan administrator for a written explanation. If you do not receive a satisfactory response, contact a lawyer.

DEFINED BENEFIT PLANS Defined Benefit Plans set forth a promise to pay a specific amount of money per month upon retirement–$800.00 a month at age 65, for example. The amount of monthly retirement income is usually determined by a formula based on years of service and earnings. The employer makes an annual cash contribution to the pension fund based on estimates of what it will cost to pay benefits in the future.

DEFINED CONTRIBUTION PLANS Defined Contribution Plans require the employer to deposit a certain amount of money annually into an individual account of each employee. The amount in the account will change depending upon investment gains and losses, including interest and dividend payments. At retirement, the employee receives whatever monies are in the account in a lump sum.

EARLY RETIREMENT Pension plans generally require that participants reach a certain age, such as 62 or 65, before they can begin receiving a full retirement pension. However, most plans permit early retirement and receipt of monthly income at a younger age, such as 55, 60, or 62, but at a reduced monthly rate. If you are terminated, you may, depending upon your age, still be eligible to receive reduced early retirement benefits. You should check the amount of pension reduction or penalty for early withdrawal. Sometimes it may be to your advantage to defer receiving retirement benefits until age 65.

VESTING Employees have no legal right to any benefit until they are vested. Vesting means the individual's "interest" in the plan is non-forfeitable and cannot be taken away. Vesting occurs after an employee has worked a minimum period of time as set forth in the plan. Federal law requires 100% vesting:

- After five years with no vesting prior to five years service; or

- Under a three-to-seven year schedule, where a percentage is vested each year and 100% is vested after seven years.

You are always 100% vested in the funds which you have personally contributed to the plan through payroll deduction or otherwise. Being 100% vested, however, does not mean you are entitled to 100% of the full and final pension benefit you would receive if you worked until age 65. Being vested only entitles you to receive at normal retirement age the full amount of benefit accumulated at the time of your termination.

There is no law giving you the right to receive the vested amount of your pension in a lump sum. Instead, payment will be governed by the terms of distribution set forth in the plan.

REGULATION OF PENSIONS The Employee Retirement Income Security Act of 1974 (ERISA) regulates pension plans. If your employer breaches ERISA or the terms of the pension plan, you have the right to file suit under federal law. For many violations, you must first file a claim under the internal system of appeals set forth in your pension plan before you can go to court. If you have questions concerning pension plans, you should consult a lawyer, accountant, actuary, or other pension expert.

HOW TERMINATION AFFECTS YOUR PLAN All employer contributions to your retirement or savings plans will cease upon termination. You will most likely be unable to make additional contributions. If you have not been employed for very long with your employer, you might lose all benefits that had been built up, unless you are vested.

Check the terms of the plan to see if there is any event or time period which is upcoming in the near future which would permit you to qualify for a larger benefit (the date when you would accumulate another year of service, for example). Ask if there is some way for you to stay on the payroll or otherwise obtain credit for an additional year of service in order to enhance your benefits.

SAVINGS PLAN For savings plans other than pension or retirement plans, different rules apply. When you can make withdrawals from the account and the consequences of doing so are not linked to age, but to other factors such as length of participation in the plan or length of employment. If you participated in a savings plan in which your employer matched funds that you contributed, you are entitled to the amount of money that you contributed, but you may lose the employer's matching funds, depending on how long you have been in the plan.

Most savings plans do not require you to withdraw the funds in your account upon termination. The funds can remain in

➤ **FYI**

Additional information and assistance is available from the Pension Rights Center, 918 16th St. NW, Washington, D.C. 20005, (202) 296-3778.

the employer's plan, and some, such as 401(k) plans, will continue to grow through reinvestment. Again, except in rare cases, all employer contributions will cease. Whether you can continue your contributions depends on the plan.

WITHDRAWAL OF FUNDS AT TERMINATION Consider all the options before taking money out of your plan. You must decide for yourself whether you need money badly enough now to dip into your account and possibly incur a penalty. You can sometimes take all of the money out of your account with your employer and put it into a private Individual Retirement Account (IRA) without incurring a penalty and without paying taxes on the amount you take out. This so-called "roll over" must be made within a certain time period set by law. Currently, the law allows sixty days from the date funds are taken out of your company account before the funds must be deposited into an IRA. Check with your financial institution about specific accounts and the penalties associated with taking that money out early. You may also want to consult a financial advisor on how best to reinvest this money.

Sometimes your pension account contains shares of employer stock or stock in other companies. Often you are better off not selling the stock at time of termination, but rolling over and transferring the stock to your own personal IRA retirement account with a bank or stock broker.

You might want to leave your pension intact to assure yourself of a steady income at retirement. Defined benefit retirement plans, unlike savings plans, will generally not get any larger with the passage of time. At the time of your termination, you should get an estimate of what your monthly pension benefit will be when you reach the retirement age and what it would be if you began receiving the pension earlier.

Finally, remember that you will be taxed on the money that you withdraw from your pension or savings account. This tax is in addition to any penalty or reduction in benefit imposed for early withdrawal from your account.

STOCK OPTIONS

Your right to exercise stock options is most likely limited by the termination of your employment. Often, you will forfeit the right to exercise the options–that is, to purchase–shares at

> **FYI**
You will be taxed on the money that you withdraw from your pension or savings account.

the price set in the option if you were terminated for cause. If you were terminated for any other reason, the time you have to exercise the options will be very short.

MAKING SURE YOU WERE PROPERLY PAID DURING YOUR EMPLOYMENT

One aspect of your employer's financial responsibility to you includes your wages. Two federal laws, the Equal Pay Act and the Fair Labor Standards Act, require employers to pay employees in a certain manner. The Equal Pay Act requires that men and women performing substantially equal work must be paid equally. The Fair Labor Standards Act requires time and one half be paid for work over 40 hours in a week for "non-exempt" employees. The termination of your employment is a critical time to reflect on these financial matters. If you suspect that you were not paid in accordance with these laws at any time during your employment, contact an attorney or the Department of Labor to try to obtain any past amounts that may be coming to you. Time is of the essence in pursuing these claims.

CHAPTER THREE

NEGOTIATING YOUR OWN SEPARATION PACKAGE

If you believe your employer's proposed separation package is unfair, you can ask for more. You can negotiate on your own or with a lawyer. Lawyers are expensive. For negotiations, they will charge a hourly rate or take a substantial percentage of whatever increase in benefits they obtain for you. Lawyers are often confrontational and combative, sometimes injecting an unfriendly adversarial tone to the proceedings. Employers may resent your bringing an "outsider" into what they regard as a "family" controversy. You may not want to jeopardize an otherwise good and long standing relationship with your former employer by retaining an aggressive lawyer to engage in protracted and hostile negotiations. On the other hand, "once you are dead, you can only get deader"–meaning that when you have been badly treated, or wrongfully discharged and are down and out, you have little to lose by being assertive. In addition, you may be too distraught, anxious, angry, and emotional to properly conduct negotiations on your own. Furthermore, many terminated employees lack the confidence, patience, objectivity, aggressiveness, or experience necessary to successfully confront employer representatives who deal with such matters on a daily basis.

If there is a substantial amount of money at stake and if the employer is being grossly unreasonable, you should retain counsel to negotiate. If the employer is asking you to sign a release of all claims in exchange for severance, and you believe the employer has violated the law, you should retain a lawyer to negotiate. Your right to sue for violation of an employment law is an extremely valuable right and should not be bargained away lightly.

If you choose to negotiate alone, you might want to consider using a lawyer behind the scenes as an advisor or coach. You should urge the employer to be reasonable because if they aren't, you will be forced to bring in an outside lawyer. One technique is to consult a lawyer in advance to get general

➤ **FYI**

WARNING: Not all the suggestions described in this chapter will be successful in every case. Sometimes the employer will refuse to negotiate and an employee is just stuck with "No" for an answer. This chapter gives employees some tools to increase their bargaining power when they try to negotiate for themselves. An attorney, however, is skilled in negotiating techniques and may be able to obtain a better deal than you could on your own.

➤ **FYI**

If there is a substantial amount of money at stake and if the employer is being grossly unreasonable, you should retain counsel to negotiate.

advice, negotiate first by yourself, and then, if unsuccessful, bring in the lawyer to negotiate and see if s/he can do better. After you have reached agreement, the employer will present you with a severance settlement release which, in all events, you should have reviewed by a lawyer.

If the circumstances of your leaving the company are unique or unusual, you may be able to obtain a better severance package than that provided by a company plan. Employers are sometimes willing to provide a special severance package to a long-term employee, an employee for whom the layoff is a particular hardship, or an employee with legitimate complaints about the fairness or legality of the discharge. If you have been the victim of a mass layoff or a legitimate downsizing, however, it is unlikely that you will be able to obtain an individually tailored severance package.

When you are terminated for any other reason, or if you think your employer unlawfully discriminated against you in choosing you–as opposed to someone else–for the layoff, you may be able to obtain more severance pay than is provided for in the company's standard plan. In any event, you will be entitled to the amount set forth in your company plan. Even if your company does not have a policy or practice of giving severance pay, you have nothing to lose by asking.

WHO HAS THE AUTHORITY TO NEGOTIATE?

Negotiate with someone with decision-making authority. It does no good to try to negotiate with your supervisor if your supervisor has absolutely no ability to control how much severance you will receive. Human resources personnel are also unlikely to feel comfortable in making an exception to the terms of a company policy or plan.

Keep going up the chain of command until you find someone with the authority to commit to a deal. If you have a choice, talk to someone you know is sympathetic to your situation.

HOW TO NEGOTIATE

Negotiations are a ritual, like a dance, involving many steps. There is no short cut to reaching an agreement. You must be

---

QuickCheck

Consider Before Negotiating

✓ *Should you or an attorney negotiate?*

✓ *With whom should you negotiate?*

✓ *Are you willing to sign a release to get more severance pay?*

✓ *What are the reasons that you are entitled to extra compensation?*

✓ *What is most important to you: money? continuing your benefits? outplacement assistance? a good reference?*

✓ *How will you be taxed on the pay or other items you receive?*

✓ *Is payment of severance pay mandatory, as set forth in the company rules, or is it discretionary?*

✓ *Could you lose the "standard" severance pay by trying to get more?*

patient. Do not let the employer bully you into making a quick decision. Tell the employer you need time to review and discuss any proposed agreement carefully and fully with your lawyer, family, and financial advisors. Do not be intimidated by the employer's warning that you must sign a release by a certain date. Most of the time the employer will be willing to extend the deadline.

There is always a risk, though a very small one, that the employer will pull its last offer off the table. Some employers will play "hard ball" and refuse to increase their offer, particularly in the event of a mass layoff where a major change would undermine the company's standard package and create bad precedent. But most employers will reinstate their last offer even though a deadline has passed because they want the matter resolved as much as you do.

HAVE A REALISTIC GOAL AND TARGET. Do not give the employer your bottom line during the first negotiation session. Compromise will make a "win-win" solution possible. Eventually both sides will have to give in a little. To give yourself some room for compromise, ask for more than you expect. However, asking for an unreasonable amount will merely sour the negotiations.

GET INFORMATION. ASK QUESTIONS. Show the employer you are serious about achieving your goals and willing to take risks to succeed. Be persistent. Do not be discouraged. Get help from friends and allies within the Company. If the employer says "take it or leave it," you must think of creative ways to end the impasse, without necessarily capitulating. Learn about the past practices of the company. Request that you be treated at least as well as other similarly situated employees.

STRESS THE FAIRNESS OF THE PACKAGE YOU PROPOSE. Point out the realities of the job market and how difficult it might be for you to find a similar position. Guilt can be a powerful motivator. Don't be embarrassed or ashamed to tell the company of the economic hardships you face, the harm done to your family, the bleak future, and the massive dollars and cents damages you will suffer in lost income, lost fringe benefits, and lost pension.

➤ **FYI**

Do not let the employer bully you into making a quick decision.

INCREASE YOUR BARGAINING POWER

Employees have more bargaining power than they realize. Employers are fearful of bad publicity. They don't like disgruntled former employees contacting higher ups, members of the board of directors, the IRS, or the media. They are concerned about the adverse effect of unfair terminations upon the current workforce and upon employee morale. They would like to end controversy and have terminated employees go away quietly and happily.

If you are a victim of a reduction in force, have an excellent work record, many years of service, and your termination was not based on poor performance but rather a bona fide job elimination, your chances of obtaining a good package are increased, particularly if yours is a "deep pocket" employer that can afford to be generous.

Your bargaining power is not increased merely because you believe the dismissal was unfair. You will have to convince the employer that the injustice is gross, egregious, and possibly illegal. Hopefully, the employer will realize it is better to quickly pay a fair severance package rather than undergo the embarrassment, aggravation, expense, and uncertainty associated with protracted and unpleasant negotiations.

Employers are frequently willing to pay a price, through expanded severance and benefit packages, to achieve a quick resolution of your dissatisfactions. Where there may have been a violation of law or gross injustice, tell the employer you are considering legal action. Employers prefer dealing with an employee without a lawyer. Make it clear that if the employer is unwilling to be fair, you will seek legal representation.

You should, however, stress that you want to avoid litigation and seek to avoid the legal fees, delay, and expense of a lawsuit. Do not threaten that if you do not receive extra money you will report the employer to the press or to government authorities. Extortion is a crime. In addition, do not declare war on the employer too early. If you are too confrontational and too hostile, the employer may become defensive and refuse to negotiate further.

Finally, you should know that if you have been discharged for misconduct, your chances of obtaining a good severance package are extremely poor unless you are a top executive.

➤ **FYI**

Caution:

Do not threaten that if you do not receive extra money you will report the employer to the press or to government authorities. Extortion is a crime.

Stress Your Strengths

Make the most of the leverage you have in negotiating. You might be wondering why your employer would negotiate with you about severance after just having fired you or accepted your resignation. There are many reasons employers pay extra money to departing employees. First, you may have a strong claim that your discharge was unlawful. If you do, it is in your employer's interest to provide you with a generous severance package in exchange for a release, in order to avoid the risk of a future lawsuit. Even without the threat of a legal claim, there are other strengths in your position. For instance, if you have been with the company for a long time and/or have made significant contributions to the company, you should be entitled to a fair severance package.

Realize you have something to sell in negotiation. First of all, you are a selling "a release," an end to the possibility of a legal proceeding and substantial damages for the company. Remember, most companies are fearful of jury trials and want to avoid litigation. Second, you are selling a "non-disparagement" agreement in which you promise not to speak ill of the company. Third, you are promising to go "quietly." The employer benefits by your not stirring up trouble, damaging the morale of the current workforce, or causing extra expense and time consuming distractions. Remember that negotiation is a two-way street. Ideally, both sides should be satisfied with the final outcome. Focus on the needs and desires of the employer as well as your own goals.

➤ **FYI**

Negotiation is a two-way street.

How Much Can You Expect To Get?

Knowing what a "standard" separation package is can be helpful to you in deciding on how much severance you will accept. Recent surveys show that senior executives usually receive at least twelve months of severance pay. Mid-level executives get six to twelve months severance pay, but at junior levels it could be as little as three to six months, with greater amounts for very long service employees who are over forty. Mid-level managers usually receive six months salary and not less than one week for each year of service. Exempt professionals frequently receive three months salary or one week for each year of service, whichever is greater. Many experts say that a good rule of thumb is a month's salary for every $10,000 in salary.

Non-exempt, hourly, and blue collar workers do not fare so well. They usually receive no more than one week's pay for each year of service and frequently much less. Two weeks pay is still the practice for many small employers.

What is a fair settlement of a wrongful discharge claim? This depends upon the likelihood of success in court, the potential damages, the underlying equities, the legal issues, the bargaining power of the parties, and the desire of the parties to settle out of court. Sometimes one year's pay plus attorney fees is considered a fair settlement of a case with a 50% chance of success.

Some employers become angry at terminated employees who ask for more than they are offered. When pride, politics, and arrogance prevent a rational review of a proposal or claim, even the best negotiator cannot obtain a fair resolution. Then the only alternatives are to take the employer's last offer or turn the matter over to an attorney.

GET CREATIVE

REDEFINE THE TERMINATION

RESIGNATION As discussed in more detail in Chapter One, you may decide to offer a letter of resignation if you are being involuntarily terminated. A resignation may make it easier on you when you attempt to find a new job. However, remember that if you resign, you may hurt any claim of illegal treatment.

EARLY RETIREMENT Most pension or retirement plans require employees to be a certain age before the employee can begin drawing the maximum pension payment per month. Some plans permit what is known as early retirement. This means that an employee is permitted to draw monthly pension payments before reaching the age specified in the plan for eligibility for full benefits. An employee who takes an "early" retirement does not draw the maximum amount per month permitted by the plan. Generally, the amount that can be withdrawn is reduced in proportion to how long before normal retirement age the employee begins receiving payments. If your employer's pension or retirement plan permits

➤ **FYI**

If your employer's pension or retirement plan permits early retirement, you should investigate whether you qualify and whether your involuntary termination can instead be treated as a voluntary early retirement.

early retirement, you should investigate whether you qualify and whether your involuntary termination can instead be treated as a voluntary early retirement.

Become a Consultant

Sometimes, it is advantageous both for the employer and employee to enter into a consulting agreement after the end of regular employment. The employer may need the employee's expertise, contacts, etc., and the employee can obtain additional income that may not interfere with other employment.

A "no-show" consulting agreement is possible. The employee need not show up for work and is paid to be "on call." If the intent of the consulting agreement is simply to create a method for payment of severance and not to actually have the employee continue providing labor for the employer, the employee should ensure that the severance agreement is not worded in such a way as to impose mandatory obligations on the employee. Otherwise, the employer could stop payment for alleged non-performance

Defer the Effective Date of Termination

Ask to defer termination by an extended "notice period" or simply continued employment for a fixed period of time (such as 90 days after notice of dismissal). With the last day of employment delayed, you will be paid longer before you get the standard severance package. This option is especially helpful to employees who are close to vesting in a benefits plan such as a 401(k) plan or a retirement plan.

❖ Make A Note

An extended notice period will give you the advantage of still having a job while looking for a new position.

Convert Unneeded Benefits to Cash

As part of a separation package, some employers offer outplacement services, job training classes, assistance in writing resumes and learning the job market, continued medical coverage, or tuition reimbursement for classes designed to help employees get back in the work force. If you think that you do not need this assistance, you may be able to trade the cost of such programs for additional severance pay.

On the other hand, benefits such as outplacement services, job training, tuition reimbursement, and/or medical coverage can be extremely valuable to some employees who have lost their jobs–more valuable than severance pay. If your employer does not offer any of the services mentioned above, you can request that your employer pay for outplacement or training through an agency you select. Depending on the circumstances of the termination, your employer may have an interest in seeing you re-employed elsewhere. For example, if you are leaving your employment because of "mutual' difficulties, requesting helpful outplacement is reasonable. If your company terminated you unlawfully and you are able to prove it in court, the company will be liable for all the wages that you lost because of its conduct. Thus, your company wants to see you re-employed, if only for the self-serving desire to reduce any amount it might have to pay in the future. Furthermore, employees who obtain good, secure, replacement jobs are less likely to sue in the first place.

Remember that income designated as "severance pay" is taxable. You should consider suggesting creative ways to avoid taxes such as payments for tuition reimbursement, outplacement services, medical insurance, pension benefits, and/or medical expenses. Interest free loans and negotiated sales of company property such as computers and company cars may also be tax free transactions. You should, however, consult a tax advisor if you are engaging in this type of negotiation with your employer. If the employer pays to settle a claim of wrongful dismissal or discrimination, sometimes a portion can be allocated to punitive and emotional damages which are not "wages" and therefore should not be subject to the current 7.65% FICA (Social Security and Medicare) deductions.

EXPUNGE DOCUMENTS IN YOUR PERSONNEL FILE

Sometimes there is derogatory information in your personnel file. You should request that the employer destroy the unflattering, unfavorable documents. Employers will often agree to seal and not open your file except for just cause or business necessity after prior notice to you. Thus, you can prevent or limit the disclosure of material relating to alleged misconduct or poor performance from being revealed.

CHAPTER FOUR

UNEMPLOYMENT COMPENSATION: YOU ARE ENTITLED. OR ARE YOU?

Every state has an agency that provides temporary benefits to persons who lose their jobs through no fault of their own. The unemployment compensation system is very similar to an insurance policy purchased by your employer. Your employer pays premiums into a state fund. If you become unemployed through no fault of your own, you apply to receive money from the insurance-like fund to assist you until you can find another job.

Each state has its own system for accepting applications. If you don't know where to apply, look in the telephone directory under state services for "unemployment compensation" or "employee services" (sometimes referred to as "Bureau of Employment Services"). It is also a good idea to call ahead to find out the hours during which applications are taken and the information you will need to bring with you.

Under current law, all applicants for unemployment compensation must serve a "waiting week." Since you cannot get benefits for the first week of unemployment that occurs after you file for benefits, you should apply as soon as possible after your job ends, even if you are not certain of your eligibility. Depending on how long you worked before losing your job, you can collect benefits for up to 26 weeks.

Sometimes, but not always, an employer will contest a terminated employee's eligibility for unemployment compensation. Whether you receive unemployment compensation depends on a number of factors.

WHY WERE YOU TERMINATED?

You are entitled to compensation if you lost your employment through no fault of your own. The states use different standards in determining fault. In some states, an employee who engaged in willful misconduct is deemed ineligible to

QuickCheck

Unemployment Compensation Eligibility

Once you have established to the unemployment office's satisfaction that you were terminated without just cause, you must follow their rules to the letter to remain eligible for benefits.

Procedures vary from state to state, but all require you to:

✓ *File a claim for benefits every week or as your state requires.*

✓ *Look for work during the benefit period and keep good records of your contacts as instructed.*

✓ *Remain available for work.*

✓ *Accept "suitable" employment.*

receive benefits. In other states, an employer need show only that it had "just cause" for terminating an employee.

Under the first standard, an employee who is a poor performer and made many costly mistakes at work would still be entitled to benefits, since his inability to perform the job is not "willful misconduct." Under the second standard, which looks at whether the employer had a good reason to terminate an employee, an employee's substandard work and errors would provide the employer with cause to fire the employee. Whether your state uses a "just cause" standard or the more lenient "willful misconduct" standard may have a bearing on whether you receive unemployment.

A "faultless" termination would involve a company which has downsized and eliminated the employee's position for economic reasons. The employee did not do anything wrong, and there was no "just cause" for the termination. Although the employer may have had a valid business reason for its decision, the individual employee was not at fault and so is entitled to unemployment compensation.

Breaking company rules or violating company policy can constitute "fault" or just cause for termination. Doing personal business on company time, behaving rudely to a customer or client, or failing to show up for work without excuse can all be just cause for termination.

Each case is different. Just because your employer cites some rule violation as the reason for your termination does not necessarily mean that you were fired for "cause" or misconduct, and that you won't be entitled to unemployment compensation. You have nothing to lose by filing for unemployment benefits and letting the state decide whether to pay your claim or not. Note that you also have appeal rights if the claim is denied, as discussed below.

WHAT IF YOUR EMPLOYER CONTESTS?

If your employer believes it had good cause to terminate you, it may file a response stating why you should not get benefits. The unemployment office makes an initial determination, usually within a week, based on your application and the employer's response. When the right to benefits is disputed, one of the parties will generally appeal this initial determination.

➤ **FYI**

If you show at the hearing that you were fired without good cause, you will be entitled to back benefits, but only for those weeks in which you filed an application for benefits

An administrative hearing will then be held, which can be months after the appeal is filed. A referee will question the parties and witnesses to make a determination on the claimant's right to benefits. If you show at the hearing that you were fired without good cause, you will be entitled to back benefits, but only for those weeks in which you filed an application for benefits.

You should consider contacting an attorney if your employer contests your unemployment. While you are not required to have an attorney represent you at an administrative hearing, legal representation can be important, especially if you believe that you were unlawfully terminated and are contemplating a lawsuit. The hearing can provide a preview of the employer's defenses to your claim.

People often believe that when they are initially denied benefits, re-applying every week is useless or unnecessary. This is not true. If you plan to appeal the denial of benefits, you must continue to file requests or applications for benefits and meet all of the other requirements for obtaining benefits. Be sure to pay attention to the deadlines for filing appeals.

DID YOU QUIT?

If you quit your job, you are not entitled to unemployment compensation unless you quit for a good cause. "Cause" here means some incident or situation that would lead a reasonable employee in that situation to quit. The situation has to be pretty bad before you are justified in quitting. Ordinarily, you must give your employer the opportunity to correct the intolerable condition.

Examples of "good cause" for quitting may include the employer's refusal or failure to pay the employee earned wages, an unsafe working environment, repeated and severe verbal or physical harassment, or a demand by your employer to engage in conduct that you know is illegal. Before you quit, you must give your employer an opportunity to rectify the situation. Certain changes in your job are not considered good cause for quitting. For example, simply being demoted, with a decrease in pay, is generally not considered "cause" for quitting. On the other hand, a demotion from manager to janitor would probably be grounds for quitting, as would removing all of your responsibilities and giving you no real work to do, especially if accompanied by a dramatic reduction in pay.

➤ **FYI**

If you quit your job, you risk being ineligible for unemployment compensation. However, you should still apply for benefits, because the state may agree that you had good cause to quit. In any event, you have nothing to lose by applying.

DID YOU RECEIVE SEVERANCE PAY?

If you received severance pay from your employer, the severance is considered income and may offset any unemployment compensation to which you are entitled. Salary continuation, when you stay on the payroll for a certain number of weeks after you stop working for the company, will usually make you ineligible for unemployment for as long as the employer continues to pay your salary. If your employer pays you severance all at once in a "lump sum," you may or may not be entitled to benefits. If the lump sum is just up-front payment of a number of weeks of your pay, the agency may treat the payment like salary continuation. You will be ineligible for benefits for the number of weeks of severance you received.

You should apply for unemployment compensation even if you are receiving severance. You should begin the paperwork immediately. When and if your severance runs out before you find another position, you can simply send in a request for compensation and the original administrative steps that you took will speed up the process of payment.

ARE YOU A UNION EMPLOYEE?

Employees who are on strike are ordinarily not entitled to unemployment compensation. Employees who are locked out by the employer are entitled to benefits. Unions often have a strike fund that is used to partially offset the loss of wages from a strike. Sometimes there is a dispute as to whether the activity in question is a strike or a lockout. If you have any doubt, file for compensation.

HOW CAN YOU MAKE THE BEST OF THE SYSTEM?

- Know and follow the rules. To receive compensation, you must meet all of the eligibility requirements of the state in which you reside. This means taking care to follow all the proper procedures. Retain copies of all documents that you give to the Bureau, and request copies of all other documents in your file.

- Fill out the application completely.

- Be on time for all appointments. Waiting is better than being told to come back another day.

- Look for work. At a minimum, make the number of applications required to maintain your eligibility for benefits.

- Keep detailed records of your job search. Record the date, name of the company, how you applied (mail, telephone, or in person), the name of anyone at the company that you spoke with, and whether you received a response to your application.

- Be available for work in your area during the benefit period stipulated in your state. For instance, if you take a week-long vacation, you will not be entitled to unemployment compensation for the week that you were out of the job market. By being out of your regular area of residence, you made yourself "unavailable' for work in your area.

- To continue receiving benefits, you must also be physically able to work. If this becomes an issue in your case, your options will depend on the nature of the medical problem. It may be necessary to obtain medical evidence of your ability to work, if this is being challenged by the state or your employer.

If you relocate permanently to another state, you are generally still eligible for benefits if you are actively looking for suitable employment in that state. However, as indicated above, states interpret the requirements for unemployment eligibility differently. Before permanently relocating, you should contact the unemployment offices in both your current and future states of residence and/or an attorney to determine the effect that relocation will have on your eligibility.

Don't refuse "suitable employment." In order to receive unemployment compensation funds, you must not refuse an offer of a "suitable" job. Whether the particular job is suitable depends on a number of factors such as the type of work, the pay, the distance from your home, and the shift you will be working.

A suitable job is one that is reasonably equal, even though not identical, to the job you had before, even if it pays less and involves less responsibility.

PROVIDING INFORMATION

You should be clear and concise in writing the explanation about why you are no longer employed. For example, state that you misunderstood directions, if you did. If you made a mistake, say so. Inform the office if you tried to avoid the mistake or rule infraction cited by your employer, and how you tried. Make sure that you inform the unemployment office if you deny the reasons set out by your former employer for your termination.

CHAPTER FIVE

PUBLIC ASSISTANCE

Being a member of the working world instills a sense of pride in employees, and justifiably so. When employment ends, many people lose that feeling of self-esteem. In its place, they develop a stubborn resistance to assistance from others, which they also call "pride." Don't fall into this trap. You have every right to, and should, make the most of all resources available to you, including public assistance. The very purpose of public assistance is to enable people to subsist until they can get back on their feet. There is no shame in requesting or accepting assistance during the very difficult period of unemployment.

With the recent overhaul of the welfare system, public assistance will vary greatly from state to state. Some of the most common forms of public assistance include food stamps, subsidized housing, medical care, and special programs for meeting the needs of infants and newborns and people with disabilities. Contact your local health and human services department to find out what programs are available and the eligibility requirements. Especially if you have children to take care of, you must exhaust all means of subsistence until you can find another job.

CHAPTER SIX

HEALTH INSURANCE

CONTINUATION OF COVERAGE

One of the most devastating effects of job loss is the loss of medical insurance. A federal law, known as COBRA (Consolidated Omnibus Budget and Reconciliation Act) has provisions that assist some employees in keeping their health insurance coverage even after they lose their jobs. COBRA's main provisions under current law are set out below.

Your employer must have 20 or more employees. If your employer employs fewer than 20 people, COBRA does not apply. However, many states have their own laws requiring employers to allow terminated employees to continue medical insurance coverage. Even if your employer is not large enough to come under COBRA coverage, your employer may still employ a sufficient number of persons to be subjected to state law requirements. Your state's department of insurance can provide this information.

For eighteen months after your employment ends or until you become eligible (whether you sign up or not) to participate under another plan, your employer must permit you to continue to participate in its group health insurance plan with the same coverage you had before termination.

NOTIFICATION

Coverage is not automatic. You must elect coverage by notifying your employer that you want to continue, or "elect," to remain in the plan. The law requires your employer to inform you within 30 days of the right to elect this coverage. You then have 30 days after receiving the employer's notice to send something in writing to your employer stating that you want to continue coverage.

To avoid a lapse in coverage, you should not wait for the notice from your employer. Elect to continue as soon as you can. If you don't, your coverage may cease and the insurance

---

❖ **Make A Note**

COBRA Facts

Law applies to companies with 20 or more employees

Employees must pay their own premiums

The benefits remain the same

Employees fired for gross misconduct do not qualify

Employees must notify their employers in writing that they wish to continue coverage

Coverage is limited to 18 months following termination

company can refuse to pay your bills. Your only recourse will be to sue your employer for damages for not telling you about your right to elect this coverage.

PREMIUM PAYMENT

When you elect to continue under your employer's plan, you, not your employer, pay the premiums, which can be over $500.00 per month for family coverage. In fact, your employer can require you to pay up to 102% of the premium. The 2% is for administration costs. You must send the premium to your employer, not the insurance company, every month or your coverage will lapse.

When you send a written notice to your employer that you want to continue coverage, include a check for the first month's premium, the amount of which can be obtained from personnel or your insurance company. Once your check has been cashed, your coverage is verified. If the company is taking the position that you are not entitled to coverage, the company must return the check to you. If you cannot get anyone to tell you what the premium should be, state that fact in the letter and specifically request this information. Take all the steps you can to get this coverage and document your efforts. It is even a good idea to send your election request and check by certified mail so you will have proof that it was received.

GROSS MISCONDUCT

If you were fired for "gross misconduct," you will not be eligible under COBRA. However, there is nothing to prevent you from negotiating for COBRA rights and notifying your employer in writing that you want to elect COBRA continuation. Since it won't cost your employer anything, you may win this one. Although the risk of being denied continued insurance because of gross misconduct is very slight, you should be aware of this provision.

FAMILY COVERAGE

Your children and/or spouse have a right of their own to continue coverage. Even if you think you don't need continuous coverage for yourself, your dependents are eligible for coverage independent of you until they become eligible under

QuickCheck
COBRA
To Do List

✓ Notify your employer in writing that you want to continue your health insurance.

✓ Find out the premium amount and the date your employer pays monthly premiums to the insurer.

✓ Include a check for the first month's premium with the notice.

✓ Verify that your employer cashed your check.

✓ Confirm with your insurance company that your coverage is in effect as soon as you receive your canceled check.

✓ Continue to send premiums for the month in which you desire coverage at least five days before the date on which your employer sends its premiums to the insurance company.

another plan. In such a case, your dependent or spouse must elect the coverage. If the premium for family coverage is too costly, but you can manage single coverage for a child or spouse who may need it, you can convert your existing policy to ensure their continued benefit.

You must decide whether you can afford to continue coverage. If you anticipate significant medical care for yourself or your family throughout the year, continuation may be crucial.

PORTABILITY

The Health Insurance Portability and Accountability Act (HIPAA), effective July 1997, makes it easier for many employees with preexisting medical conditions to obtain health insurance when they change jobs.

The law assures that an uninsured individual who seeks group health insurance will not be charged a higher premium than others in the group due to past or present medical problems. Furthermore, an individual may only be denied coverage for a preexisting condition for a maximum of twelve months. If one has been insured continuously for the twelve months prior to new coverage, she may not be excluded for a preexisting condition at all. If she has been covered for fewer than twelve months, the preexisting condition may be excluded for the number of months she was not covered, with a maximum of twelve months.

HIPAA assures employees of small businesses that a group will not be denied coverage due to one employee's past or present medical conditions. The law also affects individuals leaving group for individual coverage. The amount of time one was previously covered will determine whether he will qualify for individual coverage regardless of past or present medical conditions.

If you are changing jobs or insurance, be sure the new law is being applied to your plan, and be sure that you are receiving the appropriate benefits.

➤ **FYI**

Other Insurance

Normally, company benefit plans provide that coverage under insurance programs other than health insurance ceases as of the date of termination. Long- and short-term disability insurance and life insurance plans often permit an employee to convert to an individual policy after termination. Check your policies to determine whether you can take advantage of any conversion rights and to find out the deadlines for making a decision on conversion.

PART III

TERMS OF EMPLOYMENT

CHAPTER SEVEN:
What Rules Protect You If…

CHAPTER EIGHT:
Contracts and Promises

The right to continue employment free from arbitrary discharge depends on your legal relationship to your employer. Union employees and others with written employment contracts for a definite duration enjoy greater protection from dismissal than most non-union employees. Employees of federal and state governments usually have greater rights than those of private, non-governmental employees.

Part III gives an overview of the rights that apply in your employment situation if:

- You Are a Private Sector Employee

- You Are a Union Employee

- You Are a Government Employee

- You Are an Independent Contractor

- You Work for a Temporary Employment Agency

Part III also addresses important legal matters such as:

- What Is a Contract?

- What Is an Enforceable Promise?

- The Covenant of Good Faith and Fair Dealing

Chapter Seven

What Rules Protect You If...

...You Are a Private Sector Employee

In most states, the law presumes that private sector employees are employed "at will." The employment-at-will doctrine is that both employer and employee can end the employment relationship at any time without notice or reason. This means that your employer has the right to terminate your employment at any time, for any reason, or for no reason at all or for a bad reason, so long as the reason is not illegal–even if your performance has been outstanding. The other side of the "at will" coin is that you, as an employee, can quit your job for any reason at any time. You cannot be forced to work for an employer. You don't have to give your employer a reason for quitting.

The presumption for most non-union, non-governmental employees is that employment continues only at the will, whim, and discretion of the parties. If you are fired from your employment without just cause, you will be entitled to unemployment compensation benefits, but nothing more. Because of the employment-at-will doctrine, an unfair or unjust termination, without more, does not necessarily mean that your employer has done anything illegal.

Being fired because your boss just doesn't like you, or wants to hire her cousin to take your job, or has set impossible standards without giving you a chance to prove yourself, doesn't mean that your employer has necessarily done anything illegal. None of these bad motives alone is illegal. Also, the fact that you have worked hard for many years and were a good performer does not, standing alone, protect you from termination.

Most people believe an employer has a legal duty to treat employees fairly. Many people think an employer cannot fire an employee without just cause. Unfortunately, the general law is to the contrary. Because of the "employment-at-will" doctrine, employees have no general protection against unfair treatment. There is no "just cause" protection for non-union, non-government employees in the United States.

This situation is now the exception in most highly industrialized countries. For example, all the countries of Western Europe have legislation prohibiting employers from discharging workers without just cause. In this country, the state of Montana, Puerto Rico, and the Virgin Islands have statutes prohibiting unjust termination. However, as of this writing, no other states have similar laws protecting employees. As a result, each year thousands of employees are terminated unfairly and have no legal remedy to correct injustice.

There are noteworthy exceptions to employment-at-will. Some commentators have stated that the at-will doctrine has been drastically eroded, and that the exceptions are now so numerous as to have "swallowed the rule." The presumption of at-will employment can be rebutted by the relationship between a particular employer and employee. For example, there may be an employment contract which forbids unfair or arbitrary discharges. Many federal and state statutes place restrictions on the right to discharge. There are many laws forbidding various kinds of discrimination and other forms of wrongful discharge. For example, you cannot be fired solely because you are a woman. You cannot be fired because your supervisor does not like your religion. You cannot be fired for taking time off for jury duty. These and other exceptions to employment-at-will are discussed in later sections.

...You Are a Union Employee

The collective bargaining agreement between a union and an employer determines a union employee's rights. To determine whether a certain employment decision such as termination or demotion was illegal, a union employee must first look to the collective bargaining agreement (CBA or contract).

Union employees are not employees at will. The collective bargaining agreement contains rules governing when and how discipline and discharge shall be meted out. The CBA drastically limits the employer's ability to fire employees at will. The employer must have just cause to terminate a union member's employment. The union member has an established grievance procedure to challenge the reasons for his or her termination. Union employers often are required to utilize progressive discipline and issue written warnings prior to dismissal.

Employers must permit union members to use the grievance procedure to challenge decisions made about their employment. When employers and employees are unable to agree to a resolution of the grievance, the union has the right to have the matter submitted to an impartial arbitrator for a final and binding decision. Arbitrators have the power to reinstate employees with or without backpay and their rulings are enforceable in court.

All union members have the right to see their union contract. If you don't understand a provision of the CBA, contact the union. Speak to a union representative such as a union steward, business agent, or officer. Your union exists to represent your interests in your employment rights.

...YOU ARE A GOVERNMENT EMPLOYEE

All public employees are protected from any termination that violates the United States Constitution or the constitution of the state in which they work. Frequently, an employee's rights to freedom of speech, association, or religion, or freedom from unlawful search and seizure are at issue when an employee is terminated. In some circumstances, a government employee may have a property interest or a liberty interest in his or her position which cannot be taken away by the government, except through due process. Due process means generally that the governmental employer must give you notice of the charges against you and an opportunity to answer those charges before you are terminated from employment. If the reason given for your termination is one that would stigmatize you, jeopardizing future employment prospects, you have the right to a "name clearing" hearing.

A governmental employer may, however, establish work rules to ensure the efficient operation of the agency or branch of government or to maintain the public confidence in elected officials. Sometimes these rules place limitations on a public employee's speech or conduct. Such limitations are lawful if the government's interest in creating the rules outweighs the interest of the individual. If the speech or conduct disrupts the efficient operation of the government or would compromise the integrity of the office in which that person works, the employee may be fired.

Most public employees who are in the civil service cannot be terminated unless the employer has just cause and the termination serves to advance the purposes of the agency. Non-civil service employees of the government have less protection from discharge, but they may have other legal protections. There may be a special statute that prohibits their termination without cause or the employee may have a contract with the governmental agency prohibiting such terminations.

Federal civil service employees who believe that they were terminated without just cause, who are in the "competitive service" and who have passed a one-year probationary period, or who are in the "excepted service" and have completed two years of service in the same or similar position, can appeal their terminations to the United States Merit Systems Protections Board (MSPB). The appeal must be filed within 30 days of the effective date of the termination. Employees who do not meet these criteria may still be permitted to appeal a termination by filing a claim with the U.S. Office of Special Counsel if they believe the termination was in retaliation for whistleblowing. If they believe that the termination was discriminatory based on age, sex, religion, disability, race, color or national origin, they must contact an Equal Employment Opportunity (EEO) counselor in their employing agency within 45 days of the termination notice. Most states have similar administrative bodies to hear appeals from employees who are part of the state civil or classified service.

➤ **FYI**
Public employees who are union members and are covered by a labor agreement may also have the separate or alternative right to arbitration.

Certain categories of public employees do not have protection from unjust discharge. Political appointees, employees serving "at the pleasure" of the governmental unit, policy-making employees, fiduciary employees (those exercising independent discretion and who hold a special position of trust), or employees who serve in other positions that require special political loyalty may be terminated without cause or for political reasons.

...You Are An Independent Contractor

If you are a true independent contractor, you are not an employee. Most federal and state laws protecting employees from discrimination do not apply to self-employed, independent contractors. When a company does not retain the right to control and supervise the individual's time, work performance, method of work, job activities and working conditions, there usually is no employment relationship. In determining the independent contractor issue, courts also often look at whether the individual is truly in business for himself or whether as a matter of economic reality, he or she is solely dependent on the company.

If you are an independent contractor your right to benefits and compensation derives solely from your contract with the company. You have no rights which the law gives to employees because of the employment relationship. For example, you are not entitled to overtime under the Fair Labor Standards Act. You are not entitled to the medical insurance, pensions, and other fringe benefits accruing to employees covered by a union labor agreement or non-union company policy covering employees.

Generally, the independent contractor relationship can be terminated at the will of either party without notice unless the contract specifically provides otherwise. Some state laws provide that the covenant of good faith and fair dealing prevents a company from a bad faith termination of the contract.

The compensation of independent contractors is not subject to withholding taxes or deductions for social security. Many companies misclassify employees as independent contractors in order to avoid the legal obligations of employers to employees. Merely because you have signed a paper agreeing to be an independent contractor, is not determinative of your status. If you have been mislabeled as an independent contractor, but in fact retain the indicia and characteristics of an employee, you should consult a lawyer.

...You Work For A Temporary Employment Agency

An employee of an agency, leasing, or staffing company that provides temporary personnel is not normally considered an employee of the worksite employer. However, there are many occasions when the worksite employer is considered a "joint employer" who is indeed responsible for discriminatory or other wrongful acts committed by its supervisors. The right of temporary contract employees to compensation and benefits derives from their relationship to the staffing company, rather than the worksite employer. Most temporary leased or contract workers have no job security and no fringe benefits. An exception is that the Internal Revenue Code requires that a qualified pension plan cover leased employees for each year of service in which they work at least 1,500 hours.

Chapter Eight
Contracts and Promises

What is a Contract?

A contract is an oral or written agreement between two or more persons to take or refrain from taking some action. A legally enforceable contract is one in which both (or all) parties to the contract provide something of value to the other party or parties to the agreement. For example, if you take your car into a repair shop to be fixed, you ordinarily enter into a legally enforceable contract with the shop. The repair shop agrees to fix your car, which is a value to you. You agree to pay for the work performed, which is a value to the business.

To create an employment contract, the employer must make a specific offer and there must be acceptance of the terms of the offer by the employee. Normally the employee accepts the offer by remaining on the job and continuing to work. In addition, there usually must be a meeting of the minds or mutual intent that the promise be binding.

Not all agreements are enforceable in court. For instance, if your neighbor wins the lottery, and, in a fit of generosity, promises you that he is going to treat you to breakfast in the morning, there is an agreement for your neighbor to take you to breakfast. If he breaks his promise and doesn't take you, you can't sue in a court of law. You did not provide or agree to provide your neighbor anything of value in exchange for the promise of breakfast. To be legally enforceable, a contract must contain an exchange of value (or, in legal terms, "consideration").

If one party to the agreement breaks (or "breaches") the terms of a contract, the other party can file a lawsuit to have the court order the other party to live up to the agreement or to pay the other party for any monetary loss or damages incurred because of the broken contract.

Every person who works for wages has at least one express contract with his or her employer. By entering into an employment relationship, you agree to perform specified work for your employer. Your employer agrees to pay you for your work. If your employer does not pay you, your employer has broken this most basic of employment contracts.

WRITTEN CONTRACTS

Written contracts are, of course, the most easily recognized employment contracts. They usually contain specific terms and conditions of the employment relationship, such as duration, pay, and responsibilities. These contracts are signed by both employer and employee. Employees most likely to have individual contracts include athletes, entertainers, and high-level executives. If you have a written contract for a fixed term, for example, two years, the law requires that the employer have "just cause" for termination.

Employer handbooks, policy manuals, letters of agreement, memoranda of understanding, letters reflecting a job offer or other written statements of the employer's policies or rules may also be considered contracts. Whether such writings are enforceable contracts depends on the facts and circumstances of the particular case. For these types of writings to be considered legally enforceable contracts limiting the employer's right to terminate the employee at will, the document must contain language which shows that the employer and employee did not intend an at-will relationship.

Review your employer's policies or written rules to see if they contain any statements about termination or discharge. Check all manuals issued by your employer from the date you were first employed to the date of your termination. Check also for promises of job security. Statements of an employer's policy of retaining your employment unless you engage in certain prohibited conduct may sometimes be considered limitations on the employer's right to fire you "at will." A written policy that there will be no terminations without just cause may be enforceable as a contract.

If you had a written agreement which was broken by your employer, you have the right to sue your employer for any economic damages you sustained. Such damages can include the wages and benefits you will lose as a result of the broken contract or expenses incurred in locating another job. Before going to court, however, you should confront your employer and try to negotiate a peaceful settlement of the matter.

QuickCheck

Enforceable contracts can sometimes be found in:

✓ *Employer handbooks*

✓ *Policy manuals*

✓ *Letters of agreement*

✓ *Memoranda of understanding*

✓ *Letter reflecting a job offer*

ORAL CONTRACTS

Agreements that are not in writing may sometimes be binding. There are certain limitations on the enforceability of oral contracts that do not exist for written contracts. Oral contracts are difficult to prove. But do not automatically assume that you have no enforceable agreement with your employer just because it is not written down, especially if others heard the statements.

IMPLIED CONTRACTS

Express oral and written agreements between an employer and an employee are not the only type of contract recognized by courts. In the employment setting, certain terms of employment may be implied by your employer's conduct, policies, and practices. These are known as implied contracts.

Progressive discipline policies, statements made about job security, and even your employer's past history of requiring just cause for termination can all be evidence of an implied contract between you and your employer that you will not be fired without cause. Again, you must closely examine your employer's policies, rules, handbooks, practices, and any statements made to you by managers to see if you might have an implied contract with your employer regarding the circumstances under which you can be terminated.

WHAT IS AN ENFORCEABLE PROMISE?

Under certain conditions, a promise by an employer may be enforced in a court of law, even though the employee did not give or promise something of value in exchange for the employer's promise. To make a promise enforceable in the employment setting, you must show the following:

- A specific promise by your employer to take some action;

- That you relied on the promise;

- That your reliance on the promise was reasonable;

- That your reliance on the promise caused you harm or was detrimental to you in some way; and

- That to avoid unfairness, the promise should be enforced.

❖ **Make A Note**
Disclaimers

Employers usually seek to negate the idea that their policies are binding contracts and generally include disclaimers in their handbooks. A disclaimer usually states something like, "This handbook is not a contract, and all employees are subject to termination at the will of the company." or "These rules are for guidance only. Your employer retains the right to terminate you at any time with or without cause." If your handbook has a disclaimer, the handbook might not be binding or enforceable in court.

However, if you received an earlier version of the handbook that did not have the disclaimer, you might be able to rely on the earlier manual to prove you had a contract.

The best way to illustrate this concept, known as "detrimental reliance" or "promissory estoppel," is by example. A salesman, Archie, has worked for 22 years for a manufacturer. He is recruited by a competitor and offered a job with a higher base salary and commission structure. Archie offers his resignation to his current employer. The company president assures Archie that his job is secure, that he has always been an excellent employee, and that if he continues to perform well, he will have a job with the company for at least five years. Archie is satisfied with that answer and informs the competitor company that he is staying at his current job. Two months later, the sales manager accuses Archie of complaining about him to the president. "You're fired," the manager tells him. Two days later, he receives a letter, signed by the president, confirming his termination.

In this scenario, the employer specifically promised Archie that his position with the company was secure for five years as long as he continued to perform his job well. Based on the president's assurances, Archie refused the employment offer at the other company. Archie's reliance was harmful or detrimental because he could have had a higher paying position with another company. Unfairness would certainly result if the promise were not enforced. If you believe that your employer broke a specific promise to you, you may be able to enforce the promise and recover damages if there was detrimental reliance. You should certainly consult an attorney if you think this doctrine might apply to your situation.

THE COVENANT OF GOOD FAITH AND FAIR DEALING

The parties to a contract have a duty of "good faith and fair dealing" towards each other. As a general rule, the duty does not limit the employer's right to dismiss an employee. However, a very few states do apply the covenant to a contractual employment relationship and permit a dismissed employee to sue for bad faith discharge.

PART IV

A CRASH COURSE IN EMPLOYMENT LAW

A complex web of federal and state laws prescribe what employers can and cannot do regarding existing and potential employees. These laws fall into several broad categories which include discrimination, breach of employment contract, retaliation, tort, and benefit rights. If you are going to protest your termination, with or without legal assistance, you must know the specific law or regulation your termination violated.

CHAPTER NINE:
*Federal Laws That
Protect Workers*

CHAPTER TEN:
State Law Protection

CHAPTER ELEVEN:
*Were You
Discriminated
Against?*

CHAPTER NINE

FEDERAL LAWS THAT PROTECT WORKERS

Federal law prohibits employers from taking action against any employee on the basis of the following: race, religion, color, national origin, sex (gender), age, disability, pension or benefit status, union activity, refusal to engage in unsafe activities, protesting discrimination, and lodging a complaint with a regulatory body. In addition, federal laws place duties on employers regarding wages.

THE NATIONAL LABOR RELATIONS ACT

The National Labor Relations Act (NLRA) prohibits an employer from interfering with an employee's right to belong to a union and engage in union activity. These rights include:

- The right to organize and bargain collectively. The right to be free from termination or threats of termination for union membership, for union activity, for encouraging others to organize or vote for a union at an NLRB election, or for attending union meetings.

- The right to be free from interference when engaging in concerted protected activity. Filing grievances, demanding the presence of a union steward at meetings that may result in discipline against an employee, engaging in concerted activities such as an economic strike or demands for higher wages and better working conditions, are all protected activities for which an employee may not be disciplined or terminated.

- The right to be free from coercion to join or oppose a union. If you work for a unionized employer, you are protected from discrimination and termination for refusing to join the union. You will, however, still be bound by the terms of the collective bargaining agreement that covers your unit, and you still must pay union dues related to representation in collective bargaining

➤ **FYI**

All of the federal laws referred to in this book are written laws that are collected in a series of books called the "United States Code," or the U.S.C. for short. The U.S.C. is organized into Titles and Sections for the purposes of referring to a particular law. For instance, the Equal Pay Act is just the popular name for laws contained in Title 29, Section 206. The "official citation" for the Equal Pay Act is 29 U.S.C. §206. The official citations for all of the federal laws referred to in this book are found in Appendix A.

and in grievance processes. Not joining the union simply means that you are not a card-carrying voting member. It does not deprive you of the protection of the union contract or representation by union officials.

When an employer or a union commits an act which violates any provision of the NLRA, the employer or union has committed an "unfair labor practice." The National Labor Relations Board (NLRB) is the agency charged with the responsibility to hear and investigate charges of unfair labor practices. A violation of the collective bargaining agreement is not an unfair labor practice. Therefore, the NLRB has no jurisdiction to remedy unfair discharges. Instead, the union contract itself will spell out the procedures to follow in challenging a discharge. This will usually involve some type of grievance arbitration procedure.

The NLRA also protects a union member from arbitrary and bad faith action by his or her union. If the employer violates the contract, but the union for malicious, discriminatory or arbitrary reasons refuses to assist the member in protecting union rights, the employee can sue both the union and the employer. The employee claims that the union failed in its duty of fair representation and that the employer violated the collective bargaining agreement. To prevail, the union member must prove the employer breached the contract and that the union acted arbitrarily, discriminatorily, or in bad faith.

THE CIVIL RIGHTS ACT OF 1964

The Civil Rights Act of 1964 as amended by the Civil Rights Act of 1991 protects the civil rights of all Americans. One part or "title" of the Civil Rights Act, Title VII, prohibits discrimination in employment based on race, color, religion, national origin, or sex (including discrimination based on pregnancy).

RACE, COLOR, NATIONAL ORIGIN OR SEX DISCRIMINATION

Discrimination occurs when an employer treats one employee differently from another employee when the two are similarly situated. It also occurs when an employer takes some adverse action, such as discipline or discharge, based on a bias or prejudice that the employer has against a trait or characteristic of the employee. Finally, discrimination

❖ Make A Note

Not joining the union simply means that you are not a card-carrying member. It does not deprive you of the protection of the union contract or representation by union officials.

occurs when an employer's employment decisions or policies, although seemingly neutral, adversely impact one class of persons more harshly than another.

Discrimination is illegal under Title VII, however, only when the difference in treatment or bias is based on one or more factors that the law prohibits an employer from considering. If an employment policy or decision adversely impacts a class of employees, the policy is illegal only if the class affected is a class protected by law. (These classes are often referred to in the law as "protected categories" or "protected groups.")

> **EXAMPLE:** Several persons apply for a promotion. One of the applicants, Applicant A, is an Iraqi. The employer decides to hire Applicant B because Applicant B has two more years of experience, but also because the employer fears the Iraqi employee would not be accepted by its customers. By taking the employee's national origin into account in making its decision, the employer has violated Title VII.

> **EXAMPLE:** A supervisor repeatedly over a long period of time makes demeaning remarks to an employee of Asian heritage because the supervisor doesn't like Asians. That supervisor is acting against an employee on account of that person's national origin. Such conduct is prohibited. Even if the Asian employee is not terminated, the harassment based on national origin violates the law.

Discrimination is not always based on "disparate (different) treatment" of an individual employee. Discrimination can also occur when an employer makes an employment decision which seems to be free from discrimination and based on neutral factors, but the effect of which adversely impacts a protected group more severely than a non-protected group.

> **EXAMPLE:** An employer may adopt a policy during a layoff to terminate all employees without a 4-year college degree. In this example, 25% of black employees have 4-year degrees, while 80% of the white employees do. This employer's policy results in a disproportionately large percentage of blacks being laid off from employment. Unless the employer can show a legitimate business necessity for the policy, the policy is unlawful because of its "disparate impact" on blacks, a class of employees protected from discrimination.

RELIGIOUS DISCRIMINATION

ANTI-DISCRIMINATION Title VII prohibits discrimination against an employee because of that employee's religion. An employee's religion should have no bearing on hiring, firing, or other disciplinary action. Harassment of an employee based on the employee's religious affiliation would also violate Title VII.

REASONABLE ACCOMMODATION Title VII also requires employers to provide reasonable accommodations to an employee's "sincerely held religious beliefs" unless doing so would be an undue hardship on the company. Incurring more than minimal direct or indirect expense can be considered an "undue hardship." Similarly, an employer need not change an established seniority system or violate a collective bargaining agreement in order to accommodate an employee who, for example, cannot work on Saturday. If a requested accommodation requires more than minimal change, expense, or effort, the employer may successfully argue that accommodation of the request would constitute an undue hardship.

THE AGE DISCRIMINATION IN EMPLOYMENT ACT

The Age Discrimination in Employment Act (ADEA) prohibits discrimination based on age. Persons protected are those age 40 years or older. Similar to the anti-discrimination provisions of Title VII, the ADEA prohibits an employer from treating an employee 40 or over differently than an employee under 40 because of the older employee's age. The ADEA was designed to eliminate the termination of older employees based on stigmatizing and false stereotypes about older workers, for instance, that they are less adaptable to change, are out of touch with modern technology, or slower than younger employees in doing their jobs.

Evidence of age discrimination includes age biased remarks, statistical evidence showing a pattern of older workers being disproportionately terminated, retention of less qualified, younger employees doing the same job, other older workers victimized by the same decision-maker, or replacement by a younger employee.

THE AMERICANS WITH DISABILITIES ACT

ANTI-DISCRIMINATION

The Americans With Disabilities Act (ADA) prohibits employment discrimination against individuals with a disability. For purposes of the Act, a "disability" is defined as a physical or mental condition that substantially limits a person in a major life function or functions. Only those with permanent, chronic, or long-term conditions are considered disabled under the ADA. The physical or mental condition must be more than temporary, but it does not have to be incurable. Short term disability that results from an accident or illness does not qualify under the ADA as a disability.

The ADA protects you if you currently have a disability, have a record of having a disability, or are perceived as having a disability, even if you do not.

To be considered substantially limited in a major life function, your limitation must be more than marginal, but less than debilitating. Your disability must affect a major life function more than marginally. Whether a disability is substantially limiting is determined on a case-by-case basis. There are no rigid rules that will tell you whether a particular disability is substantially limiting or not.

Major life functions include walking, breathing, caring for oneself, seeing, speaking, hearing, performing manual tasks, learning, eating, and reproducing. Working is also a major life function in a broad sense. If your physical or mental condition prevents you from working in a class of jobs or a broad range of jobs, your disability affects a major life function. If the disability prevents you from performing only a limited class of jobs, your disability may not be considered to limit you in a major life function.

The ADA also protects persons with mental disabilities that affect major life functions, for example, someone with a learning disorder, clinical depression, or schizophrenia. The ADA covers persons with an alcohol or drug addiction so long as that person is not currently using drugs or alcohol. You can't be fired because you are a recovering alcoholic. However, you can be fired for being under the influence of alcohol on your job.

> ## ➤ FYI
>
> *If your disability makes you unable to perform any work at all, you will probably not prevail under the ADA; however, you should apply for Supplemental Security Income. "SSI" provides monetary support for persons who are too disabled to work.*

Of course, like the other discrimination laws, the ADA requires that you be qualified for your job in order to be protected from discrimination. For ADA purposes, this means that you are able to perform the essential functions or elements of your job (or the one you are applying for) either with or without some reasonable accommodation. If you cannot perform the essential functions of the job no matter what accommodations the employer makes for you, you are not a "qualified" disabled person with respect to that position.

REASONABLE ACCOMMODATION

The ADA requires that employers with 15 or more employees provide "reasonable accommodation" to the known disabilities of its employees. An employer must provide the reasonable accommodations necessary to enable an employee to perform the essential functions of a job.

➤ **FYI**

If your employer terminated you because it claimed it could not provide an accommodation to your disability, see your local EEOC office as soon as possible.

The reasonable accommodation requirement under the ADA requires much more of an employer than the previously discussed accommodation requirements of Title VII for religion. Under the ADA, an employer must accommodate the known disabilities of an employee to enable the employee to perform the essential functions of his or her job unless to do so would be an undue hardship for the employer. The ADA, unlike Title VII, requires the employer to do whatever is reasonably necessary to accommodate the employee, including modifying work schedules, altering the physical workspace, providing special equipment, providing an assistant (such as an interpreter for a deaf employee) or eliminating nonessential functions of the position.

Whether any particular accommodation is an "undue hardship" under the ADA depends on many factors, including the size and financial resources of the employer. General Motors, for instance, would be expected to incur greater costs or provide a broader variety of accommodations to an employee than would a neighborhood shop owner.

If your employer terminated you because it claimed it could not provide an accommodation to your disability, see your local Equal Employment Opportunity Commission office as soon as possible. *(See Appendix B for a list of EEOC regional offices.)*

THE FAMILY AND MEDICAL LEAVE ACT

QuickCheck
Fundamental Aspects of FMLA

✓ *The right to take up to twelve weeks (60 working days) of unpaid leave during a 12 month period which may be a calendar year or a "rolling" 12-month period.*

✓ *Flexibility to take the leave as needed. For example, you can take a week off during one month, two days off the next month, and one day during the next month. The leave does not have to be taken even a day at a time; you can take off a half day every other day if that is what is medically necessary. This is known as intermittent leave and is permissible for all types of leave except for leave to care for a newborn child or a newly adopted child.*

✓ *Continuation of your medical benefits while you are on leave.*

✓ *The right to take vacation or sick leave before taking unpaid leave.*

The Family and Medical Leave Act (FMLA) requires companies with 50 or more employees within a 75 mile radius to allow an employee to take unpaid time off of work because of the birth or adoption of a child, the employee's own serious health condition, or the need to care for a seriously ill child, spouse, or parent. Employees must have been employed by the employer for at least one year and worked more than 1,250 hours in the prior 12 months to be eligible to take the leave. If you and your spouse work for the same company, you each get twelve weeks of leave, except for the birth or adoption of a child.

Except for leave taken for the birth or adoption of a child, medical necessity is the benchmark for when leave can be taken. What constitutes a "serious health condition" permitting an FMLA leave is not well defined. Illnesses, such as upset stomach, common cold, or non-migraine headaches may not qualify. If the medical condition requires hospitalization or requires bed rest under the supervision and care of a physician for more than three calendar days, the condition will most likely be considered a serious medical condition.

Your employer may require you to show that the leave is necessary. If the leave is for your own illness, your employer can require verification from a doctor that the leave is necessary. Some top level, highly paid executives can be denied the leave if the leave would disrupt the business, and in some circumstances may be denied the right to return to their former positions.

The most important protection provided by the Act is this: You cannot lose your job for taking FMLA leave. Your employer must return you to the job you left when you went on leave, or must place you in a substantially similar (i.e., nearly identical) position when you return from leave. However, your employer does not have to pay you while you are on leave. Additionally, your employer can require you to use up vacation and sick time before taking unpaid FMLA leave.

The "Anti-Retaliation" Provisions of the Federal Statutes

The federal laws mentioned above and others related to employment (for instance, the Fair Labor Standards Act) all contain provisions prohibiting an employer from taking adverse action against an employee, including terminating employment, because the employee engaged in activity that was protected under the law. Thus, an employer cannot fire you because you have filed an EEOC charge. It is also illegal for an employer to fire you for complaining about discrimination, for giving testimony or supporting someone else who claims to have been discriminated against, or for protesting conduct you think is unlawful.

The same agencies that handle claims of discrimination under the various laws also handle claims of retaliation. For example, if you file a charge of sexual harassment against your employer, it is unlawful for your employer to take any adverse action against you, including discharge, because you filed such a claim. If you are fired, you would file a charge of retaliation with the EEOC, the same agency that handles sexual harassment complaints.

The Worker Adjustment Retraining and Notification Act

The Worker Adjustment Retraining and Notification Act (WARN) enacted in 1989 requires employers with more than 100 employees to give 60 days notice that a mass layoff or a plant closing will occur. The law does not prohibit an employer from closing a plant or laying off its workforce for economic reasons. The purpose of WARN is to give employees some time to make plans for employment after the layoff or closing and to make the transition from one job to another with minimal loss of income.

A plant closing occurs for purposes of WARN when an employer temporarily or permanently shuts down one of its employment sites or facilities and 50 or more employees lose their jobs over a thirty day period. WARN defines a mass layoff as a reduction in force of 33% of full time workers or a lay-off which affects more than 500 workers, whether the 500 constitute 33% of the workforce or not. WARN applies to temporary layoffs lasting more than six months. It also applies when the requisite number or percentage of employees have their hours reduced by 50% for a period of at least six months.

An employer who does not give proper notice to employees about a mass layoff or plant closing must pay each affected employee 60 days pay. The amount paid may be reduced if the employer provided some notice, but less than 60 days notice.

In some cases, employers are excused from giving the notice. The exceptions are complicated and, unfortunately, no governmental agency has responsibility for accepting and investigating complaints of violations of WARN. If you believe that your employer has violated WARN, see an attorney immediately.

THE EMPLOYEE POLYGRAPH PROTECTION ACT

The Employee Polygraph Protection Act (EPPA) severely restricts the ability of employers to administer lie detector tests and/or use the results to make employment decisions. Under the EPPA, it is unlawful for your employer to require, request, or even suggest that you submit to a lie detector test; or to discharge, discipline, or discriminate against you for refusing to take a test, for "failing" a test you did not have to undergo, or for complaining that your employer's actions are unlawful. The employer may not use, refer to, or inquire about the results of any test that you do take.

There are narrow exceptions. Your employer may require you to submit to a lie detector test as a condition of continued employment in connection with an ongoing investigation involving economic loss or injury to the business, such as theft or embezzlement, *but only if*:

- You had access to the property that is the subject of the investigation; and

- Your employer has a reasonable suspicion that you were involved; and

- Your employer provides you with a signed statement before the test telling you the reason you are being tested; and

- You are given a written notice of your rights under the Employee Polygraph Protection Act (which includes the right to consult an attorney) and a list of the questions to be asked.

You are permitted to leave the test any time. The questions cannot be asked in a degrading or intrusive manner. You cannot be questioned about your religious beliefs, political or racial opinions, or any matter relating to sexual conduct. Regardless of the results of the test, your employer cannot take any action against you based *solely* on the results.

THE EMPLOYEE RETIREMENT INCOME AND SECURITY ACT

For the private sector, the Employee Retirement Income and Security Act (ERISA) regulates pension plans, retirement plans, and what are known as "welfare benefit plans," such as profit sharing or bonus plans, severance pay policies, or medical insurance plans. ERISA does not require an employer to have pension, retirement, or welfare benefit plans, but once an employer adopts such a plan, ERISA governs how the plan must be implemented.

ERISA law protects an employee from termination in several ways. First, it prohibits an employer from terminating an employee to prevent that employee from vesting in a pension or retirement plan, to prevent the employee from accumulating or accruing benefits even after vesting, or making any employment decision based on an employee's pension status. ERISA also makes it unlawful for an employer to terminate an employee to prevent the employee from participating in the pension plan or any welfare benefit plan. For instance, it would be unlawful for your employer to fire you so that you could no longer participate in a health care plan, based on the employer's belief (right or wrong) that some health condition of yours would raise the company's premiums. Likewise, an employer could not fire you to prevent you from obtaining a bonus or benefit that you already earned according to the employer's plan. You have a right to participate in the employer-provided plans without retaliation or termination.

➤ **FYI**

ERISA makes it unlawful for an employer to terminate an employee to prevent the employee from participating in the pension plan or any welfare benefit plan.

THE RAILWAY LABOR ACT

The Railway Labor Act (RLA) covers employees of interstate rail and air carriers. Unionized employees who are discharged may pursue grievances before Public Law Boards and Boards of Adjustment. These Boards, established by carriers and unions, perform arbitration-like functions. Employees discharged for union activity have a private right of action to sue directly in court.

THE RACKETEER INFLUENCED AND CORRUPT ORGANIZATIONS ACT

Discharged employees who are victims of crimes committed by their employer may have claims under the Racketeer Influenced and Corrupt Organizations Act (RICO). To prevail, the employee must prove a pattern of racketeering and criminal activity. Whistleblowers, victims of mail and wire fraud, and sexual harassment victims may, under certain aggravated circumstances, have RICO claims.

THE UNIFORMED SERVICES EMPLOYMENT AND REEMPLOYMENT RIGHTS ACT OF 1994

It is illegal for an employer to discharge an employee because of any obligations s/he has as a member of a reserve component of the armed services. In addition, the law prohibits an employer from discharging a veteran without just cause within one year of returning from service to his former employer.

THE CONSUMER CREDIT PROTECTION ACT

An employer cannot discharge an employee for only one garnishment of wages. However, the law does not protect an employee who has been garnished more than once.

THE JUROR PROTECTION ACT

Employers are prohibited from discharging an employee because of federal jury service.

OTHER CIVIL RIGHTS ACTS

42 U.S.C. § 1981

42 U.S.C. § 1981 guarantees that black persons and persons of other races have the same right as white persons to make and enforce contracts. In the context of employment, this means that if an employer engaged in race discrimination in terminating an employee or failing to hire an employee, the employee could sue the employer under 42 U.S.C. § 1981. Discrimination in hiring, formation of the employment contract, firing, or the ability to enforce an employment contract, can violate an employee's civil rights.

42 U.S.C. § 1983

42 U.S.C. § 1983 makes it illegal for anyone, "under color of state law," to deprive another of his civil rights secured by the U.S. Constitution and federal laws. "Under color of state law" means that a person has used or invoked some state policy or practice (and in rare cases, a law) to justify a termination of an employee in violation of the employee's federal civil rights. Section 1983 claims are often alleged by state employees who are victims of discrimination. Section 1983 also protects government employees from termination that would interfere with any of their constitutional rights.

42 U.S.C. § 1985

42 U.S.C. § 1985 makes it unlawful for anyone to conspire to deprive an individual of his civil rights, equal protection, or privileges and immunities under law. Generally, §1985 claims are brought in conjunction with §1981 and §1983 claims when more than one person is involved in making the allegedly discriminatory decision.

THE FALSE CLAIMS ACT

Federal law prohibits an employer from submitting fraudulent requests for payments to the United States government for work performed under a contract. Such fraud can take the form of inflated invoices, requests for payment for work not actually performed, or any other misrepresentation in the documentation submitted to the government for payment. Examples of employers covered by this law are defense contractors and employers submitting bills to Medicare or Medicaid.

An employee who believes that his employer is cheating or defrauding the U.S. Government may have a claim under the False Claims Act. If the employee's information proves to be true and was not already known to the government, the employee is sometimes entitled to part of the fines or repayments that the employer must make. In addition, an employee who is discharged in retaliation for complaining about fraud or for involvement in a False Claims Act investigation may have a cause of action in court.

False Claims Act cases are especially difficult. If you believe your employer is cheating the government, seek the advice of an attorney who has experience with False Claims Act lawsuits.

THE IMMIGRATION AND NATURALIZATION ACT

It is illegal for an employer to discharge legal aliens because of their citizenship or national origin.

FEDERAL ANTI-TRUST LAWS

An employee cannot be discharged because of anti-competition practices in violation of the anti-trust laws.

THE BANKRUPTCY ACT

No employer may terminate an individual solely because the individual has filed for bankruptcy under the Bankruptcy Act.

THE WHISTLEBLOWER PROTECTION ACT

This statute provides anti-retaliation protection for federal employees who report their agency's violations of law or gross abuse of authority.

THE FEDERAL CIVIL SERVICE REFORM ACT

This statute gives certain federal employees the right to contest terminations without just cause at hearings before the Merit System Protection Board (MSPB).

THE EQUAL PAY ACT

The Equal Pay Act is a federal law that prohibits an employer from paying men and women different wages or salaries for substantially similar work performed under the same working conditions. Men and women must be paid equally for performing in positions that are substantially equal in skill, effort, and responsibility.

Whether positions are equal in skill, effort, and responsibility depends on the actual duties of the persons involved. Job titles or descriptions alone do not determine whether the positions are similar. The day-to-day job duties are critical. If the jobs require the same levels of education, experience, and responsibility, the same physical or mental exertion, and the same types of work environments, the positions are substantially similar.

If there are differences in the skill, effort, or responsibility required, an employer is permitted to pay different salaries or wages for the two positions. For example, if a male employee and a female employee are both punch machine operators, but the female employee works the graveyard shift while the male employee works the day shift, the jobs are not substantially similar because they are not performed under the same working conditions. It is not uncommon or unlawful for an employer to pay a higher wage or "premium" to persons who work the less desirable shifts.

The differences in the requirements for the positions must be related to performance of the position and meaningful to the position. An employer could legitimately pay a higher salary to an employee who was certified or licensed in his or her field, while paying less to someone who is a novice or helper. An employer could not, however, justify differences in pay for skills or degrees that are unrelated to the position. For example, if a male security guard at a mall had a college degree in biology while the female security guard had only a high school diploma, an employer could not pay the two differently for performing the same position even though the male employee was better educated, since his education did not relate to the position he was performing.

There are other exceptions to the Equal Pay Act's requirements, including seniority systems and pay based on bonus or sales. If you believe you were paid less than an employee of the opposite sex even though you performed a position that was equal in skill, effort, and responsibility, you should contact an attorney to try to obtain any past amounts that may be owed to you.

THE FAIR LABOR STANDARDS ACT

The Fair Labor Standards Act (FLSA) is another federal law governing the payment of wages to employees. Two of the most important requirements of the FLSA are minimum wage and overtime payments.

The minimum wage is currently set at $4.75 per hour. It will be raised to $5.15 per hour beginning September 1, 1997. If you were paid as an hourly employee, you were entitled to be paid at least $4.75 for each hour you worked up to 40 hours per week. If your employer paid you a salary (a set amount of pay regardless of the number of hours that you work), your pay is still subject to the minimum wage provisions. When your salary is divided by the number of hours worked in the pay period, you must still receive at least $4.75 per hour. If you earn a commission or work at a "piece rate," your total pay divided by the number of hours worked still must be no less than $4.75.

In addition to paying a minimum wage, employers subject to the FLSA must pay workers time-and-a-half, or one and one-half times the employee's regular rate (as defined in the statute), for every hour worked after the 40th hour during the workweek. Under current law, the FLSA does not authorize an employer to substitute "comp time" for overtime payment. According to the FLSA, only governmental agencies can allow employees time off in place of wages for overtime. Some state laws may permit employees to substitute compensatory time for overtime pay upon request under limited circumstances.

Some employees are "exempt," that is, not covered by the overtime provisions of the FLSA. Executive, administrative, and professional workers do not have to be paid overtime if the circumstances of their employment meet certain criteria, one of which is that the employee must be paid a fixed weekly salary, not an hourly wage. However, the fact that an employee is paid solely on a salary basis, does not mean that the employee is not entitled to overtime. That will depend on the actual duties of the job.

In addition to being paid a salary, an employee must perform administrative, executive, or professional functions for the employer. These positions usually require the employee to exercise a great deal of discretion in how the job is to be accomplished, to manage or direct the work of two or more employees, to have hiring and firing authority, or to perform work that is primarily intellectual. Whether an employee is an executive, administrative, or professional employee depends on the day-to-day responsibilities, not merely job titles or even job descriptions.

Generally, if you worked in a position in which you carried out the policies of the company, directed the work of other employees, or performed a high level, primarily intellectual position requiring an advanced education, you were exempt from the requirements of the FLSA relating to payment of overtime, and you are not entitled to overtime. Otherwise, you are probably entitled to overtime pay even though you were paid a salary.

➤ **FYI**

In "close cases," you should contact the Department of Labor to see if you were or were not exempt from overtime pay requirements.

CHAPTER TEN

STATE LAW PROTECTION

Workers are further protected by state laws that guarantee additional rights or reinforce federal rights.

In our judicial system, there are two sources of law: statutory law and common law. Statutory laws are those laws created and enacted by state or federal legislatures. These are written laws contained in volumes like the United States Code or the Ohio Revised Code. Common law, on the other hand, is so-called "judge-made law." Actually, common law is state law that has developed over time. It is law, based on custom and morality, governing the conduct of citizens. Some of the state laws discussed in this chapter are common laws and some are statutory. Both types of laws are equally enforceable.

UNLAWFUL DISMISSALS

Each state has different laws regulating the employment relationship. No two states have exactly the same laws. However, most states have statutes created by state legislatures prohibiting discriminatory discharge based on race, religion, sex, national origin, age and disability. In addition, many states have specific statutes prohibiting certain kinds of discrimination not covered by federal law, for example, with respect to sexual preference or marital status.

OTHER UNLAWFUL CONDUCT—TORTS

Many states have specific statutes forbidding discharge of employees who file workers' compensation claims. Many statutes prohibit retaliation against "whistleblowing" when an employee reports criminal, unlawful, or unsafe conduct to the employer or an outside agency. Some states prohibit a company from "black listing" former employees to prevent them from getting another job.

Each state has common law rules which affect the employment relationship. We have previously discussed state common law rules forbidding breach of contracts. In addition, employers who violate common law rights and duties causing personal injury are liable for damages caused by "torts"–or civil wrongs. The preceding sections have discussed ways in which terminations violate a discrimination statute or an employment contract. The following sections briefly describe other unlawful conduct that may accompany termination and violate common law.

INTENTIONAL INFLICTION OF EMOTIONAL DISTRESS

Intentional infliction of emotional distress is sometimes referred to as the "tort of outrage." In some cases, the circumstances of termination are so cruel, intimidating, and severe that an employee suffers extreme emotional upset. In certain instances, it is unlawful for an employer to deliberately cause an employee serious emotional harm. You might have been treated unlawfully if the employer's conduct toward you was:

- Extreme and outrageous, beyond the bounds of acceptable conduct in a civilized society;

- Intended to, or could reasonably be foreseen to, cause a reasonable person serious emotional trauma; and

- Actually the cause of severe and serious emotional distress for you.

The law does not protect against "mere insult." The focus for this kind of claim is on the outrageousness of the conduct and the severity of the emotional distress that results. Being fired on the spot and escorted out of the building by security in front of all of your former co-workers is probably not enough, alone, to constitute intentional infliction of serious emotional distress. Being handcuffed without justification or being subjected to repeated racial slurs, or severe sexual harassment may constitute an "outrage" that can be remedied.

DEFAMATION

A person is "defamed" when one person communicates a lie or a makes a false accusation about another person, either orally or in writing, to a third person, which causes damage to the person's reputation. Defamation can be written or verbal. The legal term for written defamation is "libel." The legal term for oral defamation is "slander."

In the employment setting, defamation most often occurs if a supervisor or manager makes a false accusation of dishonesty or serious misconduct against an employee in front of co-workers or members of management or if an employer provides false information to a potential employer calling for a reference.

Many termination cases are potential defamation cases. Sometimes the employer states facts about work performance or competency which can be proven to be 100% false.

A company–in order to carry on its business efficiently–is entitled to what is known as a "qualified privilege" to make statements about its employees regarding discipline, termination, and references. It is not enough that your employer made a false statement about you. The person making the statements must have acted maliciously or known that the statement was false or was reckless in determining whether the statement was true or not.

❖ **Make A Note**

If you suspect that your former employer is giving out bad references, have a friend call and ask for information about you. Your friend may be able to confirm your suspicions.

If your employer simply makes a mistake in providing a reference by looking at the wrong file, for instance, you do not have a claim for defamation, even though your employer gave out false information. If your employer gives an unfavorable opinion about your work to another person, you do not have a claim for defamation unless your employer states that the unfavorable opinion was based on a fact which is not true and which damages your reputation. Opinions generally cannot be the basis for a claim of defamation.

Finally, you must prove that your reputation has been injured in order to recover for defamation. Some false statements are obviously injurious to reputation ("She stole from the company right and left") while others must be shown to have actually injured your reputation in the community.

INVASION OF PRIVACY

The "right to be let alone" protects certain private interests–such as family, medical, sexual, or other extremely personal matters–from unreasonable intrusion. Most states recognize a "right to privacy" which an employer may not invade.

Government employees have the protection of the United States Constitution, which prohibits state, local, or federal government from conducting unreasonable searches and seizures. For public employees, constitutional protection generally means that a federal or state employer cannot invade or search in areas where an employee has a legitimate expectation of privacy unless the employer has reasonable grounds to conduct the search or inquiry, or has a reasonable suspicion of wrongdoing. Some random drug testing that is not justified by safety or security reasons may be illegal.

Private sector employees have fewer safeguards than public sector employees. Some states recognize that private sector employees have legitimate expectations of privacy at work and will provide relief for employees whose privacy has been invaded unjustifiably without legitimate business necessity. Most, however, offer no guarantee of protection against reasonable searches of work areas, desks, lockers, cars, and even personal belongings, or against monitoring electronic mail and computer input and transmissions.

One exception, however, is the interception or monitoring of telephone calls if the employer knows that the call is a private call and is made with the expectation of privacy. Such conduct violates federal law. If your employer has a policy prohibiting personal calls, however, you could still be terminated for violating the employer's work rules.

Generally, state laws do not protect employees from discharge for private, off-duty criminal, political, or sexual activity. However, the right of privacy may prevent employers from some unreasonable intrusions such as unjustified surveillance of the employee, breaking and entering the employee's home, sexual harassment, or wrongful procurement of confidential medical information.

FRAUD

If your employer deceived or misrepresented facts to you, your employer has committed "fraud." To prove fraud, you have to show that a manager purposefully told you something that s/he knew was false at the time, with the intent of deceiving and harming you. You also have to show that the fraud caused you some harm, such as monetary loss.

ASSAULT AND BATTERY

The terms "assault" and "battery" are used interchangeably by many people, but each has its own legal definition. In civil (non-criminal) law, a "battery" occurs any time a person is touched by another person or object without that person's consent. An "assault" occurs when one person attempts to touch a person either with his body or an object without that person's consent. If someone swings his fist at you and misses, you have been assaulted. If someone swings at you and hits you in the face, you have been battered (again, for the purposes of civil law).

If you have been assaulted or battered by someone at work, you can sue that person for your injuries. Under some circumstances, your employer may also be responsible to you for an assault committed by a supervisor or other employee in the course of his or her duties. In the context of employment terminations, an unlawful battery can occur when a security guard forcefully removes an employee from the premises by making physical contact with the employee or shoves the employee into his or her desk or locker while the employee is trying to gather personal belongings.

Your employer can also be held responsible under discrimination laws for a battery committed by someone who harasses you on account of your sex, age, race, disability, color, or national origin if the harasser's conduct becomes physical. If you complained to your employer about the harassment before it became physical and your employer failed to stop the harassment, some states allow recovery against your employer for the physical battery.

Generally, if you are injured at work by another employee, whether your co-worker intended to injure you or not, you are entitled to "workers' compensation" for your injuries and lost work time. If an employee is seriously injured by another employee, the workers' compensation system may not provide sufficient monetary support for the loss of income, and it usually doesn't provide any compensation for "pain and suffering." If you prove that your employer is responsible for injuries sustained in an assault at work, you can recover "pain and suffering" damages and punitive damages–which might be substantial.

FALSE IMPRISONMENT

"False imprisonment" occurs when a person's freedom of movement is impeded without that person's permission and without legal justification. False imprisonment can occur, for example, if your manager calls you into his or her office and refuses to allow you to leave (by locking the door or threatening you) and then proceeds to interrogate you about workplace problems or even about personal issues. Whether you have been falsely imprisoned depends on all of the facts and circumstances of the situation, including the length of time you are held against your will, the reason for your detention, and the manner in which your freedom to leave is impeded.

False imprisonment claims, like other personal injury or tort claims, are generally brought together with a claim of wrongful discharge or discrimination and not by themselves. However, in particularly serious situations, these claims can be brought alone.

VIOLATION OF PUBLIC POLICY

Most states prohibit an employer from discharging an employee for a reason that violates the "public policy" of the state as represented by state law, constitution, or otherwise. For example, most states have laws prohibiting dumping toxic waste into lakes and streams. An employee learns that his employer has been dumping waste in violation of the law. The employee informs his supervisor about the problem, but his supervisor tells him to mind his own business. The employee then reports the company to a state environmental agency, and the employer is fined a large amount of money. When the company learns that the employee told the state agency about the dumping, the employee is fired. Permitting an employer to terminate an employee for such a reason would undermine the policy of the state against dumping toxic waste, since other employees would be afraid to report their employers' wrongdoing if they knew that the employer could legally fire them for doing so.

States vary widely in their recognition of the right of an employee to bring a lawsuit against an employer when the employee is terminated in violation of a state public policy. The past decade has seen a growing number of courts willing to accept the idea that an employee should not be terminated for doing something that advances the policy of the state or when the termination would otherwise undermine the state's policy. Commonly recognized public policy claims include refusing to commit a crime or refusing to commit perjury, exercising a civic right or duty such as jury

 **Make A Note**

An employee terminated for protesting conduct that goes against the state's policy is said to have been "terminated in violation of public policy" or to have "a public policy claim."

duty or filing a workers' compensation claim, or reporting a crime to public officials. Because of the varying interpretations of this type of claim, you should seek the advice of an attorney to find out your state's laws.

NEGLIGENCE

Most states do not impose a general duty of care upon companies concerning the employment relationship. Thus, an employer who mistreats, harasses, improperly evaluates, or wrongfully dismisses an employee is not liable for a claim of negligence. However, in many states negligent misrepresentation of material facts, negligent hiring, supervision or retention of a dangerous employee, negligent infliction of emotional distress, and negligent failure to provide a safe workplace may be grounds for a lawsuit. Separate from the question of employer negligence, an employee may be able to sue independent contractors such as doctors, polygraph examiners, detectives, and drug testing agencies for negligent performance of their duties.

INTERFERENCE WITH THE EMPLOYMENT RELATIONSHIP

Unlawful or "tortious" interference with contract occurs when one person, for his own personal benefit or to injure another for no legitimate reason, attempts to or causes the termination of the employment relationship between two other parties. If, for example, you leave one job to start another, and your former employer, without solicitation, calls your new employer and attempts to get you fired, your former employer may be guilty of unlawfully interfering with your new employment contract or relationship. Interference with contract can also occur if someone at your current employment, for purely personal and unjustified reasons, gets you fired based on some baseless accusation. You would not be able to sue your employer in that scenario, but you could sue the co-worker for interfering with your employment relationship.

CHAPTER ELEVEN
WERE YOU DISCRIMINATED AGAINST?

Many of the laws described in the previous chapter have identifiable elements that help you determine whether you might have been treated unlawfully. Discrimination claims are a little different. You might have a "gut feeling" that you were discriminated against. But how can you tell if you have a valid case? There are numerous questions that you can ask yourself to help determine whether discrimination played a part in your termination.

DISCRIMINATION CLAIMS

You are protected by the federal anti-discrimination laws only if you fall into the category or "protected class" of persons that the particular law covers. The protected class of persons differs under the various federal laws and are summarized in other chapters.

EVIDENCE OF DISCRIMINATION

DIRECT EVIDENCE "Direct Evidence" is the best way to show that discrimination occurred. Direct evidence of discrimination includes statements by managers or supervisors that directly relate the adverse action against you to your protected class status. For example, if your employer tells you that you are being let go because you are near retirement age and the company wants to go with a younger image, you have direct evidence that your protected class status (i.e. age) was the cause of your termination. This evidence can be in the form of verbal comments or statements written in letters, memos, or notes.

CIRCUMSTANTIAL EVIDENCE The likelihood of obtaining direct evidence of discrimination is extremely remote. Supervisors and other company personnel are too sophisticated and too well-trained by their own attorneys to openly express their biases and prejudices. In almost every case, an employee must rely on circumstantial evidence.

According to the "McDonnell-Douglas Test," named for a famous Supreme Court decision, a positive response to the following four questions raises a presumption of discrimination, also called a "prima facie case" of discrimination:

- Are you a member of a protected class? For example, if you are claiming age discrimination, are you 40 or over? If you are claiming disability discrimination, are you disabled?

- Were you qualified for your position? For example, if your job required you to be a licensed technician, were you licensed?

- Did your employer take adverse action against you? For instance, were you demoted or fired?

- Were you replaced by a person who is not in your protected class (or, in the case of age discrimination, someone substantially younger than you)?

The law will presume, since you were qualified for your job and then discharged in favor of someone not in your protected class, that your protected class status was the reason for the adverse action.

The "circumstantial evidence" test is flexible. It has been modified over time to avoid a mechanistic approach to discrimination cases. A person claiming discrimination who does not have direct evidence of discrimination must produce enough circumstantial evidence of discrimination to allow a jury to find that the employer acted discriminatorily. The law recognizes that persons can be discriminated against even if they were not replaced by someone outside of the protected class, for example during a reduction in force.

Positive responses to the following questions also assist an employee in marshalling sufficient circumstantial evidence to raise a presumption of discrimination:

- Were you treated differently than a similarly situated person who is not in your protected class?

- Did managers or supervisors regularly make rude or derogatory comments directed at your protected class status or at all members of your class and related to work? For example, "Women don't belong on a construction site" or "Older employees are set in their ways and make terrible managers."

- Are the circumstances of your treatment so unusual, egregious, unjust, or severe as to suggest discrimination?

- Does your employer have a history of showing bias toward persons in your protected class?

- Are there noticeably few employees of your protected class at your workplace?

- Have you noticed that other employees of your protected class seem to be singled out for adverse treatment or are put in dead-end jobs?

- Have you heard other employees in your protected class complain about discrimination, particularly by the supervisor or manager who took the adverse action against you?

- Are there statistics that show favoritism towards or bias against any group?

- Did your employer violate well established company policy in the way it treated you?

- Did your employer retain less qualified, non-protected employees in the same job?

➤ **FYI**
No single piece of evidence is usually enough to prove discrimination. On the other hand, there is no "magic" amount or type of evidence that you must have to prove discrimination.

If you answered "Yes" to the first three McDonnell-Douglas questions and to several of the questions above, you may be able to establish a presumption that your protected class status caused the adverse employment action.

COUNTERING YOUR EMPLOYER'S DENIALS

Once you establish a presumption of discrimination, consider the reason that your company gave for terminating you. In court, an employer has the opportunity to offer a legitimate, non-discriminatory reason for its conduct. This is not very difficult for an employer to do. All that the law requires is that the employer "articulate" or state a reason. It does not have to prove that it is the true reason. A company can almost always come up with some reason for the action that it took. Once the employer articulates this reason, your presumption of discrimination is gone and you will have to offer additional evidence, as discussed further below.

If the employer cannot offer a legitimate reason for your termination, the presumption remains and you have proven a case of discrimination. However, don't count on this happening. You may think, "My employer can never come up with a good reason for firing me!" Recall, however, that your employer doesn't need a "good" reason, just any reason besides your protected status. The vast majority of employers can do this.

Assuming that your employer can offer any explanation at all for terminating your employment, you must next consider whether you can prove that the reason is just a pretext, a cover-up, for discrimination. There are several ways to do this.

- Can you show that the stated reason is:

    Factually untrue?

    Insufficient to have actually motivated your discharge?

    So riddled with errors that your employer could not have legitimately relied upon it?

- Can you show that your protected status is more likely to have motivated your employer than the stated reason?

- Do you have powerful direct or circumstantial evidence of discrimination?

If you can demonstrate any of the above, you may be able to prove that the employer's stated reason is just a coverup or pretext for discrimination. The law requires you to show not only that the stated reason is false, but that the unlawful factor was the real reason, or that the employer's stated reason and your protected status both played a role in your termination.

RETALIATION CLAIMS

Most of the federal laws that protect employees' rights contain provisions that make it unlawful for an employer to retaliate against someone who engages in conduct which the law protects. Proving retaliation can be difficult. The following are key questions to be asked in considering a claim for retaliation.

WHAT IS PROTECTED CONDUCT?

"Protected conduct" includes all aspects of trying to oppose or remedy discrimination, such as filing a charge of discrimination. Examples are: threatening to file a charge; complaining about, opposing, or protesting perceived discrimination against that employee or another employee; assisting someone else in opposing discrimination; giving evidence or testimony to an investigator; refusing to engage in conduct that the person believes to be unlawful; and refusing to assist an employer (by testimony or otherwise) in discriminating. Under the Family and Medical Leave Act (FMLA), requesting or taking medical leave or protesting your employer's refusal to allow you to take leave is considered protected conduct. Even making inquiries about a certain policy or practice of the company, or about your participation in any retirement or other plan covered by the Employee Retirement Income and Security Act (ERISA), is protected conduct.

DID YOUR EMPLOYER TAKE ADVERSE ACTION?

Your employer must have retaliated against you in some way that affects the terms and conditions of your employment before the conduct is unlawful. Usually, unlawful retaliation takes the form of demotion, harassment, or termination. You must show that your job was adversely affected by your employer before you can proceed with a retaliation claim.

DID YOUR EMPLOYER KNOW ABOUT YOUR PROTECTED CONDUCT?

You must show that your employer knew that you engaged in protected conduct. This requires that the person who makes the actual decision about your job, either orally or in writing, knew about your conduct. Telling the decision maker about your conduct is the simplest way to assure that the employer knows about you protected activity. However, there are other ways that the decision maker could have learned about your conduct. Other company employees or supervisors or the Equal Employment Opportunity Commission may tell someone at your company about your protected conduct. If you cannot prove that your employer knew about your protected conduct, you will not be able to prove a case of retaliation.

EVIDENCE THAT YOUR PROTECTED CONDUCT LED TO YOUR TERMINATION

The most difficult part of a retaliation claim is showing a causal connection between your protected conduct and the adverse action taken against you. Timing can be evidence of a causal connection. If your employer fires you shortly after you file a charge of discrimination, one can infer that your protected conduct was the real reason for your termination. Other ways to establish causal connection include showing that other employees who engaged in protected activity were fired, showing that other employees guilty of the same alleged misconduct were not fired, or showing any other circumstance which justifies an inference that your termination was motivated by your protected activity.

COUNTERING YOUR EMPLOYER'S DENIALS

You can disprove your employer's stated reasons for your termination using the same kind of evidence used to show "pretext" in a discrimination case. For example, you can show that the employer's excuse is factually untrue, that it was insufficient to have actually caused your discharge, that it is simply unworthy of credence, or so riddled with errors that your employer could not realistically have relied on its stated reason. Remember, it is always going to be up to you, the employee, to prove unlawful motivation. While difficult, it is not impossible. Circumstantial evidence can be powerful in proving your case.

ERISA CLAIMS

The Employee Retirement Income Security Act (ERISA) governs the administration of pension plans and places certain requirements on the persons responsible for maintaining the plan to look after the interests of the plan participants. If the administrators or trustees of the plan use plan funds for uses other than the benefit of the plan participants, their conduct has violated ERISA and any plan participant can sue the administrator or trustee for violation of their fiduciary duty to participants.

ERISA contains anti-discrimination provisions as well. An employer is forbidden from terminating an employee because of the employee's exercise of his right to belong to the plan, to vest in the plan, and to continue to accrue benefits under the plan. Thus, ERISA prohibits an employer from discriminating against an employee based on the employee's status in a pension or welfare benefit plan. To prove discrimination, the same direct evidence test and circumstantial evidence tests are used, although the specific elements are modified to fit ERISA participants.

The linchpin of an ERISA discrimination claim, as it is in most discrimination claims, is proving that an employer terminated an employee because of that employee's assertion of rights under the plan or status under the plan.

PERSONS PROTECTED BY FEDERAL LAW

FEDERAL LAW	YOU ARE A MEMBER OF THE PROTECTED CLASS IF YOU ARE:
Age Discrimination in Employment Act	Age 40 or older and your company employs at least 20 persons
Americans With Disabilities Act	A person with a physical or mental impairment that substantially limits you in a major life function, and you can perform the essential elements of your job, either with or without accommodation and your company employs at least 15 persons
Civil Rights Act (Title VII)	A person of any color, gender, race, or national origin, and/or a person with a sincerely held religious belief and your company employs at least 15 persons
Family & Medical Leave Act	A person who has worked at least 1250 hours in the preceding year and has been employed by the same employer for at least one year and your company employs at least 50 persons within a 75 mile radius
Employee Retirement Income Security Act	A person working for an employer with a pension plan or any other type of plan covered by ERISA
Federal Law Anti-Retaliation Provisions	A person who engaged in "protected activity" (as defined in the specific law) [The number of employees required depends on the law violated by the retaliation]
False Claims Act	Employed by a company that contracts to do work for the U.S. government

PART V

TAKING ACTION

CHAPTER TWELVE:
*Make Sure Time
Doesn't Run Out–
Statutes of Limitations*

CHAPTER THIRTEEN:
Build Your Case

CHAPTER FOURTEEN:
See An Attorney

CHAPTER FIFTEEN:
*Pursue and Exhaust
All Administrative
Remedies*

CHAPTER SIXTEEN:
Going to Court

CHAPTER TWELVE

MAKE SURE TIME DOESN'T RUN OUT– STATUTES OF LIMITATIONS

❖ Make A Note

Most statutes of limitations in employment cases begin to run on the date of notification of termination rather than the date of termination.

The "Statute of Limitations" is the law containing the period of time in which a claim under a certain statute has to be filed. Every law giving you the right to sue in court has a statute of limitation, or time limit, that goes along with it. These deadlines must be strictly followed if you wish to protect your right to seek redress for wrongful termination. You must take action on your claim within the applicable period or you will be forever barred from enforcing your rights.

FEDERAL LAWS

Several federal administrative agencies are responsible for investigating complaints that federal employment law was violated. Where you must go and how long you have to get there depends on the nature of the employer's unlawful conduct. The chart on page 100 provides basic guidelines to assist in determining where to go for help and gives the time limitations currently in effect. (Remember that laws can and do change over time.)

If a federal law was enacted after 1990 and contains no specific statute, the federal statute of limitations is four years for filing a court suit.

STATE LAWS

DISCRIMINATION CLAIMS

If your employer has fewer than 15 employees, your employer is not covered by the federal laws prohibiting discrimination. Most states, however, have their own laws prohibiting discrimination. If you believe you have been discriminated against on the basis of sex, race, color, religion, age, national origin, or disability (and in some states, sexual orientation or family/marital status), you must file with your state's civil rights or human rights agency, usually within 180 days from the date of the discriminatory act. Sometimes you can skip the filing with an administrative agency and sue directly in court.

If you want to file a claim or charge of discrimination, you need to contact your state's civil rights agency listed in your phone book (or the phone book of the nearest large city) under state agencies for "human rights" or "civil rights" or "equal employment". You might have to make several calls before you reach the right place. Remember, you are racing against the clock to get a claim filed on a very important matter. Don't be discouraged–keep pursuing your rights.

TORT CLAIMS

Defamation, intentional infliction of emotional distress, false imprisonment, invasion of privacy, interference with contract rights, promissory estoppel, violation of public policy, fraud, or assault are all "personal injury" claims, also known as "torts."

These personal injury claims are based on state law, not federal law. Each state has its own limitation period for bringing these claims. In most states, the time limit is between one and four years.

CONTRACT CLAIMS

Written contracts, oral contracts, handbook claims, promissory estoppel or implied contracts are all considered "contract claims." Once again, these types of claims are based on state law. Each state has its own time limitations for bringing a breach of contract claim in state court. Generally, claims for breach of a written express contract have a long period of time in which an employee can sue. A shorter time is set for oral and implied contracts. In most states, claimants have at least two to six years to bring a contract-like claim in court. Because of the differences in state laws, bring a claim as soon as possible after the breach occurs. In all events, consult an attorney about your rights.

Statutes of Limitations

IF YOU BELIEVE YOUR DISCHARGE WAS UNLAWFUL BECAUSE OF:	THE STATUTE OF LIMITATIONS IS:	AND THE PLACE TO FILE A CHARGE IS:
Discrimination because of race, sex, national origin, religion, pregnancy (Title VII), age (ADEA), Disability (ADA), or retaliation	300/180 days* after notification of the adverse employment action for Private Sector and State Employees	Equal Employment Opportunity Commission (EEOC)
Discrimination because of race, sex, national origin, religion, pregnancy (Title VII), age (ADEA), Disability (ADA), or retaliation	45 days after notification of the discriminatory decision for federal employees or	The Equal Employment Opportunity officer of your agency
Discrimination or a discharge without just cause	30 days after notification of the unjust decision for federal civil service employees	U.S. Merit System Protection Board (MSPB)
Complaints you made about unsafe working conditions or your refusal to perform work you believed to be unsafe	30 days	Occupational Safety and Health Administration (OSHA)
Interference with your right to organize and participate in union activities**	Six months	National Labor Relations Board (NLRB)
Violation of the Collective Bargaining Agreement (CBA)	according to CBA, usually a few days	File a grievance with employer
Your union's violation of its duty of fair representation and the employer's breach of the Collective Bargaining Agreement (CBA)	Six months	The federal district court in your state and the NLRB (for charge against union)
The Worker Adjustment Retraining and Notification Act (WARN)	***	The federal district court in your state
The Family and Medical Leave Act	Two years	U.S. Department of Labor, Wage & Hour Division, and federal court
Employee Polygraph Protection Act	Three years	Federal court or U.S. Department of Labor
False Claims Act	Six years (discharge) Three years (recovery)	The federal district court in your state
Uniformed Services Employment and Reemployment Rights Act of 1994	***	The federal district court in your state
Consumer Credit Protection Act	One year	U.S. Department of Labor, Wage & Hour Division, and federal court
Juror Protection Act	***	The federal district court in your state
Racketeer Influenced and Corrupt Organizations Act	Four years	The federal district court in your state
Fair Labor Standards Act	Two years	U.S. Department of Labor, Wage & Hour Division, and federal court
Employment Retirement Income Security Act (ERISA) Section 510	***	The federal district court in your state

*   Time limits for discrimination claims are tricky. If your state has an agency that accepts and investigates discrimination claims, you have 300 days to file a charge with the Equal Employment Opportunity Commission. If, however, you live in a state that does not have such an agency, you have only 180 days to file a charge with the EEOC. Since most states have administrative agencies that investigate claims of discrimination, most employees have 300 days to file a charge. If you are unsure about your state, make sure you file a charge with the EEOC before the 180th day and/or see an attorney immediately. Finally, because of a work-sharing agreement between the EEOC and some state agencies, at least one court has held that in Title VII cases you must file a charge with the EEOC within 240 days if your state had an agency but you did not file there. In summary, get to the EEOC or a lawyer as fast as you can after you are notified of an adverse employment action.

The EEOC will investigate your charge. If your case is not resolved, at some point the EEOC will issue you a "right to sue" letter. After you receive the "notice of right to sue," you have only 90 days to file suit in federal court or your claim will be lost forever. If you want to sue but can't find a lawyer within 90 days, go to the U.S. District Court clerk's office and request an extension of time to sue.

**   This information refers to unfair labor practices. The time for filing a union grievance claiming a breach of contract is generally much shorter. The deadline for filing can be as short as 3 days after the adverse action. Consult your CBA so you do not miss any deadlines. Deadlines for appeals from denials of your grievance are also found in the CBA and are usually very short.

*** There is no specific statute of limitations for these claims. The federal district court in your part of the state will determine, based on your state's law, what the limitations period is. If you believe you have a claim under ERISA or WARN, immediately seek the advice of a lawyer to determine the limitations period applicable in your state.

CHAPTER THIRTEEN

BUILD YOUR CASE

To build a winning case, the burden is on you and/or your attorney to gather evidence, both written and oral, that is specific, accurate, and objective. Even if you don't end up in court, you need to have a case that a judge could find credible in order for your employer to consider settling the claim in your favor.

GATHER DOCUMENTS

➤ **FYI**

Do not take documents or access information to which you have no right and are not entitled.

Gather and put in chronological order all of the documents that you can find concerning your employment–every pay stub, every memo, every handwritten note. Try, within your company's rules, to get copies of:

- Performance evaluations

- Disciplinary warnings or reprimands

- Letters of thanks or praise (from managers, customers, or co-workers)

- Internal memos

- Company bulletins

- Attendance record

- Any document stating the reason for your dismissal

- Handbooks, manuals, or other documents describing work rules, policies, and procedures

- Pension benefits and retirement plan information

- Documents related to your unemployment compensation claim

- Copies of work assignments

- Organizational charts, diagrams, floor plans, etc.

Do not take documents or access information to which you have no right and are not entitled.

IDENTIFY WITNESSES

If you think co-workers or others observed your wrongful treatment, make a list of their names, addresses, and home telephone numbers, along with a summary of what you expect them to say–whether good or bad. The "bad" or unfriendly witnesses are especially important to discuss with your attorney so that s/he can evaluate the damage they might do to your case. Forewarned is forearmed.

WRITTEN STATEMENTS

Ask friendly witnesses to give you a written statement of anything they saw or heard in person regarding your situation as soon as you decide to take action against your employer. Memories fade over time. Make sure the witnesses state only the facts of which they are personally aware and give specific examples of what they have seen themselves or what they were told directly. General statements such as, "Everyone knew that the supervisor was out to get her," are not helpful to your case. Get statements that specify the who, what, when, and where of the discriminatory or otherwise unlawful action, such as your employer's yelling at you or interfering with your work. If possible, have the written statement signed in front of a Notary Public.

The most useful witness statements are fact-intensive and unembellished by anger toward your employer or by friendship to you. They should be detailed enough so that whoever reads them–the court, an attorney, or an agency investigator–will see the "big picture."

"BIRDS OF A FEATHER"

If you know of employees who were mistreated in the same way you were, ask them for statements about the way they were treated. If your supervisor, for example, made insulting and demeaning remarks to you and other workers, get statements from the other co-workers that quote or paraphrase the remarks, give the dates on which they were made, and name any others who were present.

❖ **Make A Note**
Keep A Journal

Keep calendars, schedules of appointments, and journals. Do not mix personal and business diaries. If you are contemplating legal action, label these notes: "For Legal Purposes" or, if applicable, "To My Attorney." The notes may then be privileged and not subject to discovery or inspection by the employer. Keep track of the dates, times, places, and witnesses of events as they happen. Note who said what and to whom. Write it down while your memory is fresh.

CHAPTER FOURTEEN

SEE AN ATTORNEY

Sometimes it is difficult for the lay person to know whether the situation requires an attorney. An attorney can explain your rights and add an experienced perspective to your case. You most definitely should contact an attorney when you:

- Are considering quitting your employment because of your employer's apparently unlawful conduct;

- Do not want to, or cannot, negotiate with your employer regarding severance pay;

- Do not clearly understand your rights or are unsure of the proper action to take after your termination;

- Are nearing the end of your "statute of limitations" or deadline for filing suit and are still unsure of how or where to file a claim;

- Are being pressured to sign a complicated and lengthy "release of claims" that you do not fully understand;

- Want to file a lawsuit in state or federal court;

- Know of many other employees who want to bring the same type of claim against the same employer;

- Are dissatisfied with the EEOC's investigation of your complaint; or

- Have powerful evidence that your termination was illegal.

❖ Make A Note

Do not rely on legal advice given to you by family, friends, or even an attorney practicing outside the employment law field. Well-meaning, but bad, advice could ruin your case or lead you in the wrong direction.

FIND EXPERIENCED LEGAL REPRESENTATION

Once you have determined that you must consult an attorney, how do you go about finding one? You should get several names and talk to at least two different attorneys before selecting the one who seems best suited to your needs. You should consult with an attorney who specializes in employment or labor law. An attorney practicing in any other area, no matter how competent, won't have the experience you need to prove your claim. Employment law is a highly specialized and an ever-changing area of law with significant grey areas. Retain someone who has represented individual employees, not employers.

THE LOCAL BAR ASSOCIATION Each state has a bar association with which attorneys in the state are registered. In addition, most attorneys are members of local bar associations for the purposes of continuing legal education and public service.

Most bar associations have an attorney referral service that takes calls from the public. The service will provide two or three names of attorneys who specialize in the area of law related to their callers. The referral service does not endorse any particular attorney. The decision to consult with or retain an attorney is up to each individual.

ATTORNEYS WHO HAVE REPRESENTED YOU IN THE PAST If you have previously used the services of an attorney, s/he may be able to provide you with referrals to an experienced employment law attorney.

PERSONAL REFERENCES You are likely to get a lot of advice from family and friends about what to do in the days and weeks following your termination. Some of this advice may be helpful. Check out any lawyers suggested by your family or friends to see if they practice employment law.

THE YELLOW PAGES You can also check the Yellow Pages of your telephone directory under "Lawyers" to find the names of attorneys in your area. Look for an individual or firm that concentrates in "employment litigation" or "employment law."

THE NATIONAL EMPLOYMENT LAWYERS ASSOCIATION The National Employment Lawyers Association (NELA) is a nationwide organization of private attorneys who specialize in employment law. These lawyers work on behalf of individuals who have employment problems. NELA will provide you with the names of its members in your area. However, NELA cannot give you legal advice, represent you, or control the amount or type of fees that NELA attorneys charge. You can write to NELA at 535 Pacific Avenue, San Francisco, CA 94133.

➤ **FYI**

If you cannot locate or cannot afford an attorney, contact your local bar association, Legal Aid Society, or the local chapter of national organizations like the National Association for the Advancement of Colored People, the Women's Legal Defense Fund, the American Association of Retired Persons, and the American Civil Liberties Union. (See Appendix C).

Working With an Attorney

The law governing employment relations does not contain many hard and fast rules about what conduct is or is not legal. There are few black or white answers to legal problems. When you first talk to an attorney, do not be frustrated if the attorney is unable to tell you whether you have an airtight case. Also, do not be surprised if the lawyer you talk with agrees that there has been an injustice, but says that the law provides you with no legal recourse.

No attorney will be able to tell you whether you will win a case, even if your evidence is strong. Most of the time, the lawyer will point out the probabilities for success as well as the weaknesses in your case that could make the chance for victory at trial a slim one. Employment cases are difficult to win, expensive, distracting, and time consuming.

THE INITIAL CONSULTATION When you make an appointment to see an attorney, you should make sure you know how long the meeting is expected to last, how much the attorney charges for a consultation, and what information you need to bring to the meeting to assist the attorney in evaluating your case.

The first meeting is important. It will give you an opportunity to meet with either the attorney or with someone else in the firm who is specially trained to evaluate cases. You will have the opportunity to find out about the law firm and have your questions answered. The attorney will review the details of your case and explain your options, if you wish to pursue a claim.

The attorney will ask for specific facts necessary to determine whether your rights may have been violated. These facts often differ from those that you think are most important about your case. Provide the most accurate information that you can. Be truthful. Do not exaggerate or add information just because you want the attorney to tell you that you have a good case. Gathering evidence to support your assertions will be impossible if the information you give the attorney is not completely accurate. Everything that you tell an attorney in a consultation is "privileged." An attorney has an ethical and legal obligation not to disclose privileged information unless you agree otherwise.

Go to the initial meeting prepared to show your lawyer not only the injustice of your dismissal but how you think the law

➤ **FYI**

Gathering evidence to support your assertions will be impossible if the information you give the attorney is not completely accurate.

was violated. Take supporting documents such as evaluations, witness statements, evidence concerning treatment of others, and medical records. Explain what you think your employer is likely to say in its defense. Prepare a summary of your economic or financial damages.

THE CONTRACT FOR SERVICES Most attorneys will provide you with a written fee agreement. You may want to discuss the terms of the agreement even before you see it in writing. Probably no two attorneys have identical fee agreements.

ATTORNEYS FEES If you have seen an attorney to have a will drawn up or to get a power of attorney, you most likely paid a flat fee for the work, based perhaps on the complexity of the tasks (for example, $200 to draw up a simple will, or $700 to establish a trust).

Trial attorneys' fees are different. Trial attorneys usually charge by the hour for their work. Most employment attorneys charge at least $100 per hour, and often much more. For experienced trial counsel, you can expect the rate to fall between $150 and $275 per hour. Most terminated employees cannot afford to hire a lawyer at these rates. For a case that will be litigated in court, many attorneys work on a contingent basis; that is, they will perform all the work necessary and will take as their fee a percentage of any amount they recover for your case. If there is no recovery, they will charge no fee except for any "up-front" retainer and for expenses.

An attorney's "regular fee" is the amount he or she charges to perform work on a case, which is collected as the case progresses or at its conclusion.

An "engagement fee" or "retainer" is an amount that the attorney charges just to take the case. These fees are common, especially when the attorney has agreed to work on a contingency basis and cannot expect to be paid anything for work performed until the end of the case. The retainer or engagement fee may or may not be credited as part of the total fees collected at the end of the case.

"Costs" in a case are those out-of-pocket expenses that are incurred in the normal course of the case. For instance, filing a case in court requires payment of a filing fee. Such a charge is a cost that you, the client, are expected to pay. Your attorney does not pay these costs, even if s/he is working on a contingency arrangement. Other out-of-pocket expenses you will

➤ **FYI**

The most common contingency fee percentage is 33 1/3%. Sometimes lawyers will charge less if the case is settled prior to suit or without much work. Sometimes the fee is 40% or even 50% in the event a trial and appeal is necessary and depending on all the circumstances. Sometimes there is a sliding scale based on the amount recovered.

be required to pay include postage, long distance calls, travel expense, printing, copying, faxing, "depositions," court reporter attendance fees, transcription costs, subpoenas, and expert witness fees. Some of these costs can be very substantial. For example, the cost of taking and transcribing a typical deposition (and your case may involve several of them) is around $1,000.00. Lawyers expect you to pay these expenses as they are incurred and in all events when the case is settled. Be sure that you thoroughly discuss all the different fees and costs that can be expected in your case.

WHAT THE LEGAL AGREEMENT COVERS In an ordinary case, an attorney performs an investigation of the case to determine whether the case has merit. The attorney accepts the case for litigation if the facts and law support a case and will perform all the necessary steps to get your case ready for trial, an administrative hearing, mediation, or settlement without a trial. The fee agreement specifies the costs and expenses involved in this procedure.

However, after a trial or settlement, there may be more action necessary on your case, such as an appeal or efforts to enforce a settlement. Make sure you know whether these legal services are covered by the fee agreement or will be billed separately. Sometimes there are matters closely related to your court claim such as unemployment compensation hearings, administrative proceedings, and counterclaims (claims made against you). Find out if these matters are covered by the agreement.

THE WRITTEN FEE AGREEMENT Normally, fee agreements are in writing and contain information in addition to the fees and costs mentioned above. Read the fee agreement thoroughly. The last thing you want is to get into a dispute with the attorney who is supposed to be working for you. Ask questions. Make sure you understand the agreement before you sign it.

THE ATTORNEY-CLIENT RELATIONSHIP When you retain an attorney, you are seeking legal advice and legal assistance in pursuing a claim. Your attorney will tell you what participation will be expected from you. You should remain active in your case by providing information or doing whatever the attorney asks. You have hired an expert. Listen to what your attorney is telling you. Follow your attorney's recommendations.

Your attorney should keep you updated on what is happening in your case. Your attorney must consult with you about major decisions such as dropping a claim or settling the case.

Busy attorneys are difficult to reach by telephone. Don't feel neglected if your attorney is unable to return your call immediately. Usually the attorney cannot answer or return calls quickly because s/he is too busy working on an emergency matter involving a case. (Remember, it could be your case when someone else is calling.) If you can't get through by phone, send a letter, fax, or e-mail, giving the reason for your call. Many times the attorney will be able to respond to your satisfaction by having another staff person return your call.

Each party to the attorney-client relationship should educate the other. You should make sure your attorney explains to you in detail the various stages of a lawsuit. Be sure to ask questions if you have any doubts as to what lies ahead concerning discovery, settlement, trial, and/or appeal procedures.

Similarly, you must educate the lawyer about your job history, your life story, including medical, emotional, and financial problems, the personalities and practices at work, and all the incidents and details concerning your claims and damages. Write memos and letters to your lawyer outlining important incidents, conversations, and rebuttals to the employer's explanation and defenses. If you are not used to writing a lot, force yourself to do it anyway. Like many other things in life, it gets much easier with practice. And remember, your attorney is not looking for a college term paper, just an honest account of things which matter to your legal case.

➤ **FYI**

Make sure your attorney explains to you in detail the various stages of a lawsuit. Ask questions if you have any doubts as to what lies ahead.

Chapter Fifteen

Pursue and Exhaust All Administrative Remedies

For many discrimination or retaliation claims, it is not absolutely necessary to have an attorney. Employment attorneys are experienced and can ordinarily provide invaluable skills and advice in pursuing a claim, and you are encouraged to engage the services of an attorney if you possibly can. However, attorneys fees, costs, and retainers can be a financial impossibility for some. It may be, also, that an employee is unable to find an attorney to take the case, even if the case has merit. In these situations, the employee may have to go it alone.

Federal and state governments have established administrative agencies that can investigate some claims of discrimination or wrongdoing by employers. Employees who do not have (or, for whatever reason, do not want) an attorney to represent them can use these administrative channels to challenge a wrongful termination. Diligence, patience, and strict attention to deadlines are required in dealing with these agencies, but you may be able to obtain relief in a relatively inexpensive and timely manner.

In some of the situations described below, an employee must go through the administrative process even if s/he has an attorney. However, if you have an attorney, your attorney will be able to assist you in filing claims and following the administrative process.

Discrimination Claims

Equal Employment Opportunity Commission (EEOC)

A person employed by a private company with 15 or more employees or by a state government (including union employees) who believes that he or she has been discriminated against or harassed based on race, color, religion, gender, national origin, pregnancy, age, or disability must file a "charge of discrimination" with the Equal Employment Opportunity Commission (EEOC). The EEOC is a federal agency charged with the responsibility for investigating claims of discrimination under the Age Discrimination in Employment Act, the Americans with Disabilities Act, and Title VII of the Civil Rights Act. The EEOC headquarters is in Washington, D.C.; regional and district offices are located throughout the United States. *(See Appendix B.)*

Unless impossible for you to do so, you should go to the EEOC office in person to complete the required forms and talk to an EEOC officer. If you absolutely cannot get to an office, you can request forms through the mail. Bring copies of relevant documents and be prepared to answer questions about your employer's address, type of business, and size; your last position; and who your supervisor was. Take the names and addresses of any witnesses as the EEOC investigator may interview them as part of the investigation.

At the EEOC office you will fill out several forms, including the charge of discrimination and an affidavit (sworn statement) stating the basis for your charge. Resist the urge to tell your life story or the entire history of your employment. Stick to those facts necessary for filling out the forms. Make sure you include every one of the acts of the employer that you believe were discriminatory and the names of other employees who you know were victims of discrimination.

The length and thoroughness of the EEOC investigation will vary. Some investigations last many months, even years. Eventually the EEOC will issue a determination. In 90% of the cases the EEOC declares there is no probable cause and no showing of discrimination. On rare occasions the EEOC will find probable cause and threaten to file a lawsuit.

Because of its huge backlog and lack of resources, the EEOC is often unable to provide adequate assistance. However, sometimes the EEOC can help you get the case settled. Sometimes the EEOC will convince a charging party to drop and withdraw charges. Occasionally the EEOC will file a lawsuit on your behalf, particularly if you are part of a large class or group of employees or there is an important legal issue at stake. After the EEOC has closed its file, it will issue its ninety-day "right to sue" notice. Thereafter, you have the right to inspect your file, by filing a request with the EEOC under the Freedom of Information Act. Often the file con-

❖ Make A Note

Don't leave the EEOC office without filling out the forms. If you have made mistakes or forgotten information, you can amend your charge later. Ask for a photocopy to take with you.

Don't let anyone at the EEOC discourage you. Be firm and insist that someone accept your charge of discrimination, even if they protest that it is too early, too late, or not a credible case.

The date you file a charge with the EEOC is important. If you don't file within the time allowed by law, you will be barred from suing in court or obtaining any kind of relief for your employer's unlawful conduct in the future.

tains important information and documents supplied by your former employer which will be of value if you intend to go forward with a lawsuit.

FEDERAL EMPLOYEES

Employees who work for the federal government or for the U.S. Postal Service who believe they have been discriminated against must make a written request for "pre-complaint counseling" with the agency's internal Equal Employment Opportunity office within 45 days from the date of the discriminatory act. Each agency or department of the government has its own internal office to investigate claims. The location of the EEO office should be posted prominently in a common area in your workplace. If it isn't, ask a supervisor or any personnel staff member to direct you to the proper office. Getting to that office within 45 days is of utmost importance. Thereafter, the agency will set up a pre-complaint counseling session and explain all of the subsequent procedures that you must follow if you wish to pursue your claim.

The guidelines set forth above for filing a charge with the EEOC also apply to charges filed with the internal EEO office for federal employees.

UNION CONTRACT VIOLATIONS

In challenging a termination that you believe violates the collective bargaining agreement, you must follow the procedures set out in the collective bargaining agreement (CBA) for filing grievances. Usually, a union steward will help you fill out the grievance form. If your union declines to assist you in filing and appealing a grievance, file the grievance or a request for arbitration yourself. Send a written statement of the grievance to your local union and to the international union as well as your employer via certified mail and request a "step one" hearing. Use your collective bargaining agreement to keep track of the time limits for filing and appealing the denial of grievances and requesting arbitration.

If the employer does not act on your grievance, continue to appeal in writing via certified mail until your appeals run out. If your union declines to arbitrate, make a written request to arbitrate yourself and file it with the company and the union.

If, in addition to the breach of the CBA, you believe that your union failed in its duty of fair representation, you must follow internal union processes to appeal the union's decision to refuse to take action on your behalf. Consult your local union's constitution and by-laws and the constitution of the international union for time limits for appealing union inaction or misconduct in handling grievances.

A claim that your union has failed in its duty of fair representation and that your employer has violated the collective bargaining agreement must be filed in court within six months of the date on which the unfair representation occurred. You must, however, attempt to exhaust all your internal union remedies and the grievance procedure before you can go to court. Filing a charge with the National Labor Relations Board (NLRB) within six months is an option, in addition to a court remedy for violation of the duty of fair representation.

UNION ACTIVITIES CLAIMS

The National Labor Relations Board (NLRB) is the government agency that enforces the National Labor Relations Act. The NLRB accepts complaints of unfair labor practices (ULP) and interference with rights protected by the National Labor Relations Act; for example, discrimination because of union activities. An employee can file an unfair labor practice charge at the NLRB, using their standard forms. *(See Appendix B for regional offices of the NLRB.)*

The NLRB can either accept the charge of a ULP or reject it. Rejection is not appealable. If the NLRB accepts the charge, it will take over the claim, investigate, and, if necessary, issue a complaint and require the employer or the union to defend itself at an administrative hearing.

CLAIMS INVESTIGATED BY THE DEPARTMENT OF LABOR

The Department of Labor, Wage & Hour Division, is responsible for taking and investigating claims of violations of the Fair Labor Standards Act, the Family and Medical Leave Act, the Employee Polygraph Protection Act, and the Consumer Credit Protection Act. *(See Appendix B for a list of DOL regional offices.)*

The Fair Labor Standards Act (FLSA) sets forth the requirements for overtime pay and minimum wages. If, following your termination, you believe that you were improperly denied overtime or otherwise improperly paid, you have two years after the violation to file with Wage and Hour Division of the Department of Labor ("DOL"). The date of a "violation" is any date on which you received a paycheck that was not in compliance with the FLSA. The DOL Wage & Hour division can recover back wages for you for up to two years prior to the date of your court complaint, or up to three years if your employer willfully, purposefully, and knowingly was violating the FLSA's requirements.

The DOL also accepts and investigates claims that an employee was terminated for questioning the legality of the employer's wage practices or for protesting the employer's failure to pay the employee the required overtime pay. A charge of retaliatory discharge must be filed with the DOL within two years of the notice of termination.

Unlike discrimination claims, claims for violations of the FLSA do not have to be brought to the DOL before an employee can proceed in court. In fact, if you file a claim with the DOL, you should contact an attorney to discuss your claim. If it turns out that you must sue in court to recover lost wages or to challenge a retaliatory discharge, you must get to court within two years of the violation. An attorney will be able to evaluate your case to determine whether you have time to allow the DOL to investigate or if you must go to court right away. The rules and time limits related to FLSA claims are complicated. Don't hesitate to get advice if you believe you have a claim.

UNSAFE WORKING CONDITIONS CLAIMS

The federal Occupational Safety and Health Administration (OSHA) ensures workplace safety. If you believe that an unsafe condition exists at your workplace, you have the right to contact OSHA and inform the agency of the problem. You do not have to give your name. Depending on the type of problem that you identify, OSHA might conduct an on-site investigation or may simply direct the employer to investigate the problem and report back to OSHA.

The Occupational Safety and Health Act protects employees from discharge for contacting OSHA, cooperating with the agency, or complaining about unsafe working conditions. If you believe you were discharged for complaints to OSHA or for complaining about any unsafe condition related to your job, you have only 30 days from the time of your termination to contact OSHA.

STATE LAW CLAIMS

Most states have fair employment practice (FEP) or civil rights agencies to administer state laws related to discrimination. These agencies are very similar to the EEOC. If your employer has fewer than fifteen persons, you probably cannot take advantage of the federal laws and must instead look to your state's laws for protection. Check your phone book for state agencies. Keep calling until you get to the right agency that will address your problem. If you are unable to find any agency to help you, you should see an attorney for assistance.

You should contact an agency as soon as possible after your particular employment problem arises. Do not wait longer than 30 days unless unusual circumstances prevent you from doing so.

OTHER CLAIMS

For non-government employees of private employers, there are no agencies, state or federal, that investigate complaints of unfair and wrongful discharge not involving discrimination. If you wish to "go it alone" on common law breach of contract and tort claims, you have no choice but to sue in court if you cannot negotiate a settlement.

Chapter Sixteen

Going To Court

It may be that after consultation, investigation, and administrative processing of your case, you decide either to sue in court by yourself or to retain an attorney to sue in court. Below are some of the characteristics and processes common to almost every case.

Risk in Proceeding Without a Lawyer

Succeeding in an employment termination lawsuit without a lawyer (called filing "pro se") is virtually impossible. Besides knowing the law (only a small portion of which has been covered in these pages) and the associated court procedures, an attorney will know what information you need to win, how to get it, how to present witnesses and documents to the court and jury, and how to prevent a company and its attorneys from using unfair tactics to win the case.

Do everything you can to find an attorney to take your case. Don't make the mistake of thinking that you can save yourself some attorneys fees by taking the case to trial by yourself. You may well end up with nothing. Worse, you might end up having to pay your employer for the expenses incurred in defending against your lawsuit. In these times of increasing "court reform," it is impossible to predict what consequences may befall an unsuccessful plaintiff in the future.

If no attorney is willing to file suit for you, it may be that your termination, while unfair and regrettable, was not unlawful. You or your lawyer may still be able to negotiate with your employer for an enhanced separation agreement and a good reference letter with a non-disparagement clause. Refer to Chapter Three, "Negotiating Your Own Separation Package," for a further discussion of this option.

➤ **FYI**

Don't make the mistake of thinking that you can save yourself some attorneys' fees by taking the case to trial by yourself. You may well end up with nothing. Worse, you might end up having to pay your employer for the expenses s/he incurred in defending against your lawsuit.

Basic Stages in the Legal Process

Complaint and Answer

The complaint is a document that you must file with a court to begin a lawsuit. The complaint contains factual assertions about your case, the legal reasons that you believe that the employer's conduct was unlawful, and your damages. You must also make a request for a jury in the complaint. In the complaint you, the employee, are called the Plaintiff. The entity you are suing (e.g. the employer and/or supervisor) is called the Defendant.

After a Plaintiff has filed a complaint with the court, the Defendant must file an answer to the complaint. In the answer, the Defendant either admits or disputes the Plaintiff's version of the facts. The Defendant may also add special reasons defending itself and may also on rare occasions file a counterclaim against you.

Discovery

After the complaint and answer have been filed, you and your attorney will begin a process known as "discovery" to obtain information about your case. Much of the information you need to present in trial to prove your claim is in the possession of your former employer and can be obtained by the discovery process. Another purpose of discovery is to prevent surprises at the trial. There are several important methods that you or your lawyer can use to get this information:

- First, you can send your employer written questions (called "interrogatories") to answer under oath.

- Second, you can send written requests (called "document requests") to your employer to provide you with certain documents, such as your personnel file, documents relating to your termination, and documents concerning other similarly situated employees.

- Third, you can request managers, human resource representatives, and others to appear in person at your office or another location to answer questions under oath (at a "deposition"). Taking a deposition requires hiring a court reporter to record and transcribe the information and sending subpoenas to the people whom you wish to depose, if they won't come voluntarily.

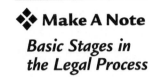

❖ **Make A Note**

Basic Stages in the Legal Process

Complaint and Answer

Discovery

Motions to Dismiss

Settlement

The Trial

Appeals

You can expect that your employer will also request discovery from you. You will almost certainly have to submit to a deposition, in which you will be required to answer questions asked by your employer's attorney. You also will probably be required to respond to your employer's written interrogatories and to produce all relevant documents or items you possess. You and/or your attorney will determine the strength of your case and what defenses your employer plans to use against you based on the information received during the discovery process.

MOTIONS TO DISMISS

Defendant employers want to avoid jury trials. They usually request the judge to dismiss the case. They will seek to persuade the court that the case is so weak it should not be submitted to a jury but should be dismissed outright. This is a routine tactic. If your case has merit and you have strong evidence, you will ordinarily be able to convince the court that your case should go to trial. Convincing the court is not an easy task in discrimination cases, however, since the issue is the intent of the employer in discharging you. Obtaining hard evidence of bad intent is difficult. In the absence of a "smoking gun," conservative judges often require massive circumstantial evidence of discrimination before they let the case go to a jury. Many cases are dismissed after they are filed, without ever getting to trial.

SETTLEMENT

It has been said that the courts in the United States do not administer justice but, rather, that they settle disputes. Many judges will encourage the parties to a lawsuit to try to settle their disputes between themselves on their own terms rather than having a dispute settled on terms set by the court or a jury.

Thus, in almost every case, you and your attorney will discuss settlement options. You will need to discuss the risks versus the benefits of continuing to trial, the chances of success, what exactly you want to accomplish with the lawsuit, the settlement value of the case, and what your "bottom line" figure is. You will need to discuss whether you should initiate or encourage settlement talks with the employer or wait until an offer is made to you.

GOING TO TRIAL

The trial of an average discrimination-termination case will normally last at least five days in court. You and the employer will have the opportunity to present witnesses and documents and to cross examine the other side's witnesses. Each side makes an opening statement and a closing argument. The court issues instructions of law to the jury which then decides the issues of fact and renders a verdict.

Cost and time are the two of the most frustrating aspects of any litigation. The expenses – not including attorneys' fees – that you can expect to incur can be anywhere from $1,000.00 to $15,000.00, depending on the complexity and duration of your case. This is money you will not recover if you lose.

Equally frustrating is the length of time it takes to take a case from complaint to trial. Depending on the court, two years could pass between the time that you first visited an attorney about your case or filed a complaint to the time that the case actually goes to trial and there is a verdict. As stated before, the chances of winning without an attorney are slim. Even if you hire an attorney, the toll that litigation takes on your finances, your time, your family, and your mental health can be overwhelming.

APPEALS

Appeals are another part of the process that can take a year or more. If you win your lawsuit, you can be sure that your former employer will appeal the decision. Even if you were awarded a large sum of money, you won't be able to get any of it until the appeals are exhausted, so long as your employer posts a bond for the amount of the verdict.

DAMAGES

Victims of illegal dismissal suffer various forms of damages. The term "damages" refers to the financial and emotional losses sustained by a person who has been unlawfully terminated. The law seeks to make the injured party whole, that is, to put the person in the position s/he would have been in, but for the unlawful acts of the employer. Normally, an employee can recover back pay–income and the value of the fringe benefits lost because of the termination–minus any amount that

❖ Make A Note

The law seeks to make the injured party whole, that is, to put the person in the position s/he would have been in, but for the unlawful acts of the employer.

❖ Make A Note

An employee has a duty to try to mitigate or lessen his losses. An employee must use reasonable diligence in seeking comparable work. Damages will be reduced where the employee, without justification, has not looked for interim employment.

➤ FYI

Many statutes permit the employee who wins a lawsuit to recover for attorneys' fees and litigation expenses.

the employee was able to earn in the interim. Back pay is measured from the date of the employment termination to the date of the court's decision. An employee has a duty to try to mitigate or lessen his losses. An employee must use reasonable diligence in seeking comparable work. Damages will be reduced where the employee, without justification, has not looked for interim employment.

Reinstatement of a terminated employee to his or her former position is considered the preferred remedy in discrimination cases. If the court deems reinstatement inappropriate, it will consider awarding "front pay," or an amount of money that the court believes is necessary to make up for the difference in pay that the employee will sustain in the future. The amount of front pay is determined by how long the court believes it will take the employee to return to the same level of pay that she had when terminated. Loss of pension plan benefits is also recoverable.

Victims of discriminatory dismissals and certain state law torts such as defamation may, in some cases, recover monetary compensation for emotional and mental distress damages. In some cases, an employee can recover for loss of reputation and loss of ability to enjoy life. In some cases, punitive damages are levied against the employer if the employer acts maliciously and with reckless disregard for the rights of the employee. The employee receives the amount of punitive damages awarded. In addition, many statutes permit the employee who wins a lawsuit to recover for attorneys' fees and litigation expenses.

Ordinarily, an employee who loses in court does not have to pay the attorneys fees and expenses of the winning employer. The employer could, however, recover its court costs, including deposition expenses, sometimes totalling several thousand dollars. Employers sometimes file motions for attorney fees when the employee has filed or maintained a frivolous lawsuit without any basis.

ALTERNATIVE DISPUTE RESOLUTION

The number of employment cases filed in court has skyrocketed in the last ten years. Court dockets are crowded. Most judges, many academics, commentators, and lawyers believe that court trials are not the best way to resolve employment disputes. There is a growing trend to explore other ways that are less expensive, less adversarial, and involve less delay.

ARBITRATION

Arbitration by a neutral third party has been the method used by labor unions and companies for many years to resolve unfair dismissal cases arising under collective bargaining agreements. Recently, many non-union companies have begun to insert clauses into employment agreements signed at the time of hire, requiring mandatory arbitration of all employment disputes, including claims of discrimination and violation of federal and state statutes.

The EEOC and most attorneys who represent employees oppose mandatory arbitration as contrary to federal policy providing a court proceeding. They argue that employees have not knowingly and voluntarily agreed to give up their rights to discovery procedures and jury trial, before a judge trained in the law, and subject to appellate review. If your employer requires you to arbitrate your claims, you should consult a lawyer immediately. Your lawyer may decide to go to court to try and stop the arbitration. If you are ordered to or agree to arbitrate, you will find the procedures more informal and less legalistic than in court. Your chances of success are slim without a lawyer. Your chances of obtaining a substantial award are less than at a jury trial.

MEDIATION

The most popular and fastest growing form of alternative dispute resolution (ADR) is mediation. The parties select a third person–usually a lawyer, retired judge, or professor– who is a trained and neutral mediator. The mediator will facilitate settlement by bringing the parties together, acting as "devil's advocate," and using various forms of persuasion, diplomacy, and sometimes manipulation. Mediators sometimes recommend a compromise settlement figure, but they have no power to require an agreement. Mediation, unlike arbitration, is strictly voluntary and does not result in a final and binding decision by a third party.

Over fifty percent of mediations end in settlement. Frequently, mediations are the catalyst leading to eventual settlement of those cases that do not settle on the day of mediation. Mediators urge the parties to explore their realistic options and come to grips with the disadvantageous uncertainty of proceeding with litigation. Cases are sometimes mediated before suit, but more often several months following the filing of suit, when both parties have had a chance to realize the downside of litigation. Ninety percent of all court cases that are not dismissed are settled prior to verdict with or without mediation. Mediation expedites matters. Employees benefit because delay, much expense, and aggravation are eliminated.

PART VI

OTHER SURVIVAL
STRATEGIES

CHAPTER SEVENTEEN:
Finding Another Job

CHAPTER EIGHTEEN:
Coping with Job Loss

CHAPTER SEVENTEEN

FINDING ANOTHER JOB

A few people who are terminated decide to retire from active work. Some withdraw from the labor market and pursue other activities. Most, however, need to find a job immediately.

Even if you ultimately win a legal action against your employer, you will face many months, possibly years, before you receive any compensation or are reinstated. Depending on the agreement you have with your attorney, you may also face extensive legal costs during the course of litigation. Do not count on a lawsuit as a source of income.

There are many books about job hunting, resume preparation, and interviewing in your local library and books stores. Your library may also be able to provide computer assistance in locating job vacancies. The following discussion summarizes the major job-hunting strategies.

NETWORKING

➤ **FYI**

Anyone you know who might have information about a job opening, or who knows someone who might have a lead about a job opening, is in your "network."

As the saying goes, "It's not what you know, it's who you know." Use every opportunity to get the word out that you are available for work. People in your profession or area of work can provide valuable information and leads. A particularly helpful strategy is to join organizations which relate to your field of work—or one you would like to be in. Not only will you increase your chances of hearing about a job opening, but you will have impressive membership information to put on your resume.

Networking is critical. Most people find employment from tips given to them by people in their network: friends, neighbors, relatives, and former customers, employers, or co-workers. Ask them for names of people who might be willing to schedule an informational interview with you. The Internet can also be a valuable source of job leads.

In addition to being one of the best job search strategies, networking is also one of the best ways to keep up social contacts and avoid isolation. Anyone you know who might have information about a job opening, or who knows someone who might have a lead about a job opening, is in your "network." You can expand your network by joining organizations outside your career field, but related to family or hobbies. People like people who are like themselves and will often go out of their way to recommend a "kindred spirit" to others in their network. Also, listing your membership in athletic, civic, artistic, parenting, or other non-employment groups gives you an acceptable way of showing prospective employers who you are as a person. If you hold a position of leadership in an organization, the employer may make positive inferences about your value to the company.

RESUMES AND REFERENCES

Professional assistance can be extremely helpful. This is especially true if you have been out of the job market and have not prepared a resume for some time.

Tailor each resume to each job application. Avoid sending a generic resume to every employer. Determine the skills that the potential employer is looking for. Revise your resume to highlight those skills. When an employer or recruiter looks at your resume, you want him or her to say, "This person has the skills we need."

Emphasize but don't exaggerate your skills. Never put anything on your resume that you can't back up with actual fact. A false or misleading entry on a resume can cause great problems down the line. It is often grounds for dismissal. There is a myth that "everyone lies on their resume." Get it out of your mind. First, it's not true. Second, it is not a very satisfactory explanation to give to an irate boss who finds you out.

If you attended college but did not graduate, do not state that you have a degree in a certain area, even if you earned all of the necessary credits in your major. Do not exaggerate your time at any company to fill in gaps in employment. If you stopped working for Employer A in 1989, and did not obtain another job until 1990, resist the urge to state that you worked for Employer A until 1990. References are important. Ask a trusted supervisor or former co-worker from past jobs where you were successful if you can use his or her name.

QuickCheck
Job Hunting

✓ Expand your network

✓ Work your network daily

✓ Update your resume

✓ Tailor your resume to fit each prospective employer

✓ Practice your interview skills

✓ Get recommendation letters from former employers and co-workers

✓ Study the job market

✓ Go to job fairs

✓ Ask for informational interviews

✓ Target your job search to your experience, expertise, and interests

✓ Use outplacement and no-fee employment services

✓ Sign up for the free or low-cost job hunting seminars and support groups

✓ Don't get discouraged!

➤ **FYI**

Steer the potential employer to those persons who will say good things about you. This may eliminate the potential employer's need to contact others who might not be so cooperative.

Pounding the Pavement

Outplacement Services

"Outplacement" refers to services offered by your employer or by an outside employment agency to assist you in finding new employment. This does not guarantee that someone will find a job for you. However, outplacement professionals can provide you with valuable assistance in preparing a resume, developing a job search plan, learning how to do well in interviews, and other skills you need to get a new job. Most outplacement firms can provide valuable assistance in uncovering the hidden job market and assisting you in making an efficient job search.

Some companies provide their laid off employees with office services such as word processing, photocopying, or just a quiet place away from home to make job search phone calls. You are encouraged to take advantage of such services if you have access to them.

Research the Job Market

Newspapers, bulletin boards, and the Internet are great sources of information about employment opportunities, as are civil service job registries, the U.S. Department of Labor, municipal and federal job telephone hotlines, postings at unemployment compensation offices, ads in trade journals, and internal postings at companies where friends work. Send your resume to as many places and people as you can. Your local Chamber of Commerce can provide a list of companies in your area and your public library can help you research them.

Many governmental agencies–local, state, and federal–have telephone job lines or civil service registries which describe the positions available in the agency at the time of your call. Federal publications list available government positions around the country and the qualifications for such jobs. The U.S. Department of Labor is also a good source of information about the employment outlook for hundreds of occupations.

Learn as much as you can about the companies you contact. The public library has a computer index of newspapers and periodicals in which the company may be mentioned. Trade journals related to the company's business can also be helpful in providing you with intelligent information to use during an interview. Send a resume even if the employer is not actively looking for employees. A "cold call" can work if you know a lot about the company and can convince the company that you can contribute to their business. It may be a cold call, but it should not be a blind call. Your chances of getting a favorable response are increased if you can direct your letter to a particular person, rather than just to "Human Resources" or the like.

JOB APPLICATIONS AND INTERVIEWS

When you fill out a job application or when you interview for a job, you will be asked for the reason that you left your last job. Have a short answer prepared for this question. Then focus the discussion on another topic–such as why you are an ideal candidate for this employer.

Be honest. Don't say that you quit when you were fired. You may get past the application stage without too much trouble. You might even successfully get through the interview. But a dishonest answer can cause significant problems later in your employment. A falsehood on an application may get you fired years later, long after you've been hired and have forgotten this little white lie. Many companies have a policy of firing persons who lied on employment applications or in interviews even if their job performance has been excellent.

State in a positive manner the reason that your last employment did not work out. For instance, instead of saying that your supervisor was incompetent or abusive, you might say that you wanted a management structure that allowed for more growth, or that you wanted more autonomy or more communication, depending on the situation, from upper management in performing your responsibilities. Turn the negative aspects of the former job into the positive aspects that you are looking for with this new company.

If you had problems getting along with your former supervisor, you might state to a new employer that, "My supervisor and I had some different ideas on how to get things done; we had a difficult time reaching common ground on things that we both knew were important to the company." If your prospective employer calls your previous supervisor and your supervisor states that the company had problems with

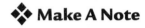

❖ Make A Note

Many companies have a policy of firing persons who lied on employment applications or in interviews even if their job performance has been excellent.

your work, you have already prepared your prospective employer for that response and explained it in a way that is not likely to harm your chances of obtaining a new position.

If you have been out of the job market for a long time, you should brush up on your interviewing skills. Many times, the interview can make or break a job prospect. When numerous applicants are vying for a small number of positions, the person who comes across the best in the interview will often be the one who gets the job.

First impressions are very important. Your dress and demeanor can play as critical a role in the hiring decision as your skills and experience. Because you only get one chance to make a first impression, it's worth reading one of the interview preparation books now available. You may be surprised at some of the observations and techniques these books provide.

EDUCATION AND TRAINING

For some individuals, termination provides an opportunity to learn new skills. We are in the middle of a technical revolution. In order to advance on the "information highway," everyone must become more educated. Find out what you should learn in order to meet the present and future needs of employers in your area and look for courses and training programs in your community. Sometimes state, local, or federal government sponsored training courses are available free or at a low cost. Consult local educational institutions, unions, and correspondence courses. Even if you don't end up needing your newly acquired skills on your next job, employers will take note that you have been resourceful during your "downtime."

CHAPTER EIGHTEEN
COPING WITH JOB LOSS

The impact of termination goes well beyond shaking a family's financial security. Job loss ranks with death and divorce as one of life's most stressful events. Strong negative emotions–anger, inadequacy, humiliation, anxiety, depression, and a host of other feelings–are not uncommon and are fully understandable following the loss of a job. Nevertheless, negative emotions are not conducive to moving forward. If you start taking them along in your personal relationships and job interviews, they can be destructive.

Job loss is a very personal experience which people handle in very individual ways. Maintaining a positive outlook may not come easily to everyone, and may require serious effort on your part. A sincere effort to follow some of the suggestions offered in this chapter, however, should be beneficial.

LET YOUR SUPPORT SYSTEM BE SUPPORTIVE

Trusted family members and friends will want to be helpful. Let them! This is not the time to push people away. Resist the temptation to close others off because you don't want to be a burden or a bore. You are still the same person with the same good traits you had before you lost your job. It is important for you and those closest to you to understand that you need time to cope and recover. Don't think you have to "go it alone" or "tough it out." It is when you shut others out that the pressures and frustrations take their greatest toll.

When "coping" doesn't alleviate feelings of grief, fear, or anger, enlist the help of family members, friends, neighbors and/or others who share your problem to establish support groups and to network. Asking for help is hard, but it is not admitting defeat; on the contrary, it is an indication of your intention to take control of your life.

QuickCheck
Coping

- ✓ Let Your Support System Be Supportive
- ✓ Stay Active
- ✓ Allocate Your Resources Carefully
- ✓ Keep Fit and Healthy
- ✓ Steer Clear of Drugs and Alcohol
- ✓ Rest and Sleep
- ✓ Join a Support Group
- ✓ Keep a Journal
- ✓ Seek Professional Counseling
- ✓ Make Time to Have a Good Time

STAY ACTIVE

Do not remain idle while you are between jobs. Inactivity aggravates negative thoughts and feelings. Institute a routine and try to stick with it.

Mental health experts agree we feel better when we are busy, especially when our thoughts are directed outside ourselves. Many people, whether or not they are employed, derive great satisfaction from performing volunteer work. For people who are out of work, volunteering has the added benefit of helping them maintain or enhance their job-related skills and may create an opportunity to learn new skills and develop new interests. Another plus is that working in a new setting and meeting new people can broaden their network.

This is also a good time to tackle projects around the house and catch up on reading. But don't let these activities distract you from getting out and doing what it takes to get a new job!

ALLOCATE YOUR RESOURCES CAREFULLY

The loss of a steady paycheck can have a devastating financial impact, even in a two-income family. Develop a budget with your family, letting each member put forward their priorities. Work out a schedule of payments with your creditors, and avoid accumulating new debt as much as you possibly can. If necessary, seek help from your local consumer credit counseling organization.

KEEP FIT AND HEALTHY

NUTRITION Nutritionists tell us that stress lowers the level of serotonin, a natural mood lifter, in the brain and that eating carbohydrates ups the serotonin level, making people feel more relaxed. Some experts also suggest that eating balanced, smaller, more frequent meals helps calm a jittery stomach. Since the body has a strong need for nourishment during stress periods, it is wise to avoid processed foods and refined sugars and eat whole foods such as fruits and vegetables instead.

Experts say that a poor diet can leave you more vulnerable to the negative aspects of stress and more susceptible to illness.

EXERCISE Exercise is one of the best ways to reduce the effects of stress. It is also a good way to improve your overall physical and mental health. Research has identified several physical changes accompanying physical exercise. These positive changes include improved functioning of heart and lungs, better muscle tone, increased energy, weight control and improved sleeping patterns.

Regular, vigorous, physical exercise is perhaps the most natural, as well as the most beneficial, method of dealing with stress and tension. A well-conditioned body is best suited to handle stress. Exercise gives the body a chance to use the hormones that stressful situations pump into the bloodstream. It also prepares the body to handle more stress by increasing strength and endurance; reducing aches, pain, and stiffness; lowering blood pressure; and increasing cardiac output by using up adrenalin which may cause muscles to tense up.

STEER CLEAR OF DRUGS AND ALCOHOL

Sometimes people who feel overwhelmed by job loss seek relief in drugs and alcohol. These substances only mask stress symptoms. They do not help you adjust to the stress itself. Turning to them can cause more stress in the long run than it relieves. Prescription medications such as sedatives or anti-depressants are sometimes helpful in balancing a person's response to stress, but must be taken only under a doctor's direction and supervision.

REST AND SLEEP

Stress often produces insomnia or fitful sleep. Some techniques people can use to put themselves to sleep include progressive relaxation (sequentially tensing and fully releasing the muscles from head to foot), deep breathing (slowly inhaling and exhaling to a count of 10), and visualization (picturing a peaceful landscape or other pleasant vista).

JOIN A SUPPORT GROUP

People who share your situation may be better prepared to listen and respond to your concerns than even the most well-meaning friends or relatives. With a group of people who understand what you are going through, you can let off steam, get feedback on your activities and give others the benefit of your wisdom. Many communities have support groups through which job seekers can exchange tips and valuable information regarding the job market. You can usually find a support group by contacting your YMCA, YWCA, or library. Sometimes employment agencies can lead you to a group that matches your needs.

KEEP A JOURNAL

➤ **FYI**

If you are planning to appeal your termination or take legal action, it is essential to make notes of the events as they occur, before your memory fades.

Some people find that writing things down provides a useful outlet and also helps them think through their problems. If you are planning to appeal your termination or take legal action, it is essential to make notes of the events as they occur, before your memory fades. Anger needs an outlet. When you are angry at someone or something and cannot express it in person, vent your anger by writing down what angers you. Don't analyze or organize the information, just let it pour out onto the paper. After you are done, take the pages and crumple them up, stomp on them, rip them up and dump them (where they won't be found). According to Helen Lerner, the author of *Stress Breakers*, "These symbolic actions, combined with the physical energy spent doing this, maximizes the emotional release."

SEEK PROFESSIONAL COUNSELING

Maintaining your emotional well being is as important during this time of crisis as securing your financial future. If–after trying these coping mechanisms–you still find yourself frequently depressed, dwelling on the past, harboring thoughts of revenge, drinking excessively, or resorting to drugs to mask your feelings, you may want to ask a professional psychiatrist, psychologist, or social worker for help.

Asking for professional help is not a sign of weakness, nor does it indicate a lack of self sufficiency. A well-trained professional can usually provide great relief while helping you to deal with your feelings and focus on the future. Your family doctor or minister can help you locate someone, as can organizations such as your local family service agency, mental health association, Jewish social services, or Catholic Charities. These and many other agencies that can offer assistance are listed in the Yellow Pages.

Get the counseling while your health insurance coverage remains in effect. If your insurance does not cover mental health treatment or if the coverage is inadequate, ask the agencies you talk to whether their fees are based on a sliding scale determined by income. Check to see if there is an employer-sponsored confidential Employee Assistance Program (EAP) which covers you.

MAKE TIME TO HAVE A GOOD TIME

Don't overlook the value of good times, either on your own or with others. Even if you think you're not in the mood, you'll probably have a good time once you are out doing something you enjoy. In his book, *Anatomy of an Illness*, Norman Cousins wrote, "It has always seemed to me that hearty laughter is a good way to jog internally without having to go outdoors." Experts say that daily laughter makes you feel happier, healthier, more self-confident, and relaxed.

EPILOGUE

You are not alone. Millions of Americans have had to cope with the realities and difficulties of unfair dismissal. We hope that the information in this book has been useful. We also hope that you will make the transition to a new job quickly with only minimal loss of income and self-esteem.

Knowledge is power. We urge you to maximize information concerning your rights. If you have questions, there are many private, public, and governmental agencies that can provide assistance. In all events, be assertive, ask questions, utilize available resources, consult experts and professionals. Know your legal rights. If you feel that your termination was illegal, be sure to see a lawyer.

Asserting your rights and seeking the best possible severance package helps build self respect, and often results in economic gain. Some employees who have been unfairly discharged seek vindication, recognition, and revenge. A large amount of money becomes the symbol of victory. Many employees tell their lawyers that "it isn't the money, it's the principle." They just want the employer to suffer, to sit up and take notice.

The period of post-termination can be a time for self-examination and for focusing on what is best for the future. To some extent, a lawsuit's focus on what went wrong at the former employer may be helpful. The downside of a lawsuit is that a lengthy involvement in the legal process traps employees into reliving the unpleasant past and impedes their ability to move forward–to get on with their lives.

Unfortunately, the reality of our economic and legal system favors corporate America. The "little guy" must frequently suffer injustice without recourse. In reality, the "better part of valor" is often to accept a severance package or modest settlement and get on with the transition from one job to another. On the other hand, our federal and state laws provide protection against most outrageous misconduct by employers. Terminated employees have every right to utilize whatever laws and remedies are available to them.

We at NERI join your family and friends in wishing you every bit of good luck and success in the days and years ahead.

❖ **Make A Note**

It has been said: "When one door closes, another one opens, but it's hell in the hallway." Often, pursuit of protracted litigation extends the period in "hell." There comes a time when letting go and forgetting the past injustice is the best course.

APPENDICES–INDEX

136 APPENDIX A

OFFICIAL CITATIONS TO FEDERAL LAWS

Citations in the United States Code where the full text of the federal laws discussed in this book can be found.

137 APPENDIX B

FEDERAL GOVERNMENT OFFICES

- Regional offices to contact for specific employment related information.

- Equal Employment Opportunity Commission (EEOC). Accepts and investigates charges of discrimination because of age, disability, race, sex, religion, national origin, or pregnancy.

- The National Labor Relations Board (NLRB). Accepts and investigates complaints of unfair labor practices of employers and unions, including illegal discharge because of union activities.

- Occupational Safety and Health Administration (OSHA). Investigates complaints of safety violations in the workplace and charges of discrimination or retaliation for reporting unsafe working conditions.

- U.S Department of Labor (DOL). Accepts and investigates complaints of violations of numerous laws pertaining to the workplace, including the Family and Medical Leave Act, the Consumer Credit Protection Act, and the Fair Labor Standards Act.

- Federal Sources of Pension Rights Information

142 APPENDIX C

NON-GOVERNMENT RESOURCES

Private organizations providing information or legal assistance on workplace issues:

- Employment Law
- General Legal Aid
- Civil Rights
- Rights of Racial, Ethnic, or Other Groups
- Sex Discrimination, Sexual Harassment, and Women's Issues
- Rights of Union members
- Pension Information
- General Information for Employees

144 APPENDIX D

SAMPLE LETTERS OF APPEAL

147 APPENDIX E

SAMPLE REFERENCE LETTERS

149 APPENDIX F

SAMPLE EEOC CHARGE FORM

APPENDIX A–OFFICIAL CITATIONS TO FEDERAL LAWS

AMERICANS WITH DISABILITIES ACT (ADA)	29 U.S.C. §12101 et seq.*
AGE DISCRIMINATION IN EMPLOYMENT ACT (ADEA)	29 U.S.C. §621 et seq.
BANKRUPTCY ACT	11 U.S.C. § 525 et seq.
CIVIL RIGHTS ACT OF 1964, (TITLE VII)	42 U.S.C. §2000e et seq.
CIVIL SERVICE REFORM ACT (CSRA)	5 U.S.C. §2301 et seq.
CLAYTON ACT (ANTI-TRUST LAWS)	15 U.S.C. § 615(a)
CONSUMER CREDIT PROTECTION ACT	15 U.S.C. §1674
EMPLOYEE POLYGRAPH PROTECTION ACT (EPPA)	29 U.S.C. §2001 et seq.
EMPLOYEE RETIREMENT INCOME SECURITY ACT (ERISA)	29 U.S.C. §1140 et seq.
EQUAL PAY ACT	29 U.S.C. § 206
FAIR LABOR STANDARDS ACT (FLSA)	29 U.S.C. §215 et seq.
FALSE CLAIMS ACT	31 U.S.C. §§3729-3731
JUROR PROTECTION ACT	28 U.S.C. §1875
NATIONAL LABOR RELATIONS ACT	29 U.S.C. §151 et seq.
OCCUPATIONAL SAFETY AND HEALTH ACT	29 U.S.C. §660 et seq.
RACKETEER INFLUENCED & CORRUPT ORGANIZATIONS ACT (RICO)	38 U.S.C. §1961-68
RAILWAY LABOR ACT	45 U.S.C. §151-188
UNIFORMED SERVICES EMPLOYMENT AND REEMPLOYMENT RIGHTS ACT OF 1994	38 U.S.C. §4301 et seq.
WHISTLEBLOWER PROTECTION ACT	5 U.S.C. §1212
WORKER ADJUSTMENT RETRAINING & NOTIFICATION ACT (WARN)	29 U.S.C. §2101 et seq.

*The term "et seq." means "and continuing." Ordinarily, when referring to an entire law and not just particular sections of it, the first section of the law is cited and "et seq." is added. "§" is the symbol for "section."

EQUAL EMPLOYMENT OPPORTUNITY COMMISSION (EEOC)

Note: This Appendix lists EEOC district offices. There may be area or local offices closer to you. If you contact a district office, ask whether there is an area or local office near you. Where there is more than one EEOC office for your state, call or write the one closest to you. If you are unable to determine your district, or for information about the EEOC's local offices, call 1-800-669-4000 or 1-800-669-3362 (Spanish bi-lingual).

ATLANTA
Citizens Trust Bank Bldg.
Suite 1100
75 Piedmont Ave., NE
Atlanta, GA 30335
(404) 331-6039

BALTIMORE
10 S. Howard St. 3rd Fl.
Baltimore, MD 21230
(410) 962-3932

BIRMINGHAM
1900 Third Ave. N., Suite 101
Birmingham, Al 35203-2397
(205) 731-0082

CHARLOTTE
5500 Central Avenue
Charlotte, NC 28212
(704) 567-7100

CHICAGO
Federal Bldg., Room 930-A
500 West Madison St.
Suite 2800
Chicago, IL 60661
(312) 353-2713

CLEVELAND
1660 West Second St.
Suite 850
Cleveland, OH 44113
(216) 522-2001

DALLAS
207 South Houston St., 3rd Fl.
Dallas, TX 75202-4726
(214) 655-3355

DENVER
303 East 27th Ave.
Suite 510
Denver, CO 80203
(303) 866-1300

DETROIT
Patrick V. McNamara
Federal Bldg., Room 1540
477 Michigan Ave.
Detroit, MI 48226
(313) 226-7636

HOUSTON
1919 Smith St., 7th Fl.
Houston, TX 77002
(713) 653-3377

INDIANAPOLIS
101 West Oh St., Suite 1900
Indianapolis, IN 46204
(317) 226-7212

LOS ANGELES
255 East Temple Street, 5th Fl.
Los Angeles, CA 90012
(213) 894-1000

MEMPHIS
1407 Union Ave., Suite 621
Memphis, TN 38104
(901) 722-2617

MIAMI
Metro Mall
1 N.E. First St., 6th Fl.
Miami, FL 33132
(305) 536-4491

MILWAUKEE
310 W. Wisconsin Ave.,
Suite 800
Milwaukee, WI 53203
(414) 297-1111

NEW ORLEANS
701 Loyola Ave., Suite 600
New Orleans, LA 70113
(504) 589-2329

NEW YORK
7 World Trade Center
18th Floor
New York, NY 10048
(212) 748-8500

PHILADELPHIA
1421 Cherry St., 10th Floor
Philadelphia, PA 19102
(215) 656-7000

PHOENIX
4520 N. Central Ave,
Suite 300
Phoenix, AZ 85012
(602) 640-5000

SAN ANTONIO
5410 Fredericksburg Rd.
Suite 200
San Antonio, TX 78229
(210) 229-4810

SAN FRANCISCO
901 Market Street,
Suite 500
San Francisco, CA 94103
(415) 744-6500

SEATTLE
909 First Ave., Suite 400
Seattle, WA 98121
(206) 220-6883

ST. LOUIS
625 N. Euclid St., 5th Floor
St. Louis, MO 63108
(314) 425-6585

NATIONAL LABOR RELATIONS BOARD (NLRB)

REGION 1: MAINE, MASSACHUSETTS, NEW HAMPSHIRE, RHODE ISLAND, VERMONT
Federal Building, 6th Floor
10 Causeway Street
Boston, MA 02222
(617) 565-6700

REGION 2: NEW YORK
Federal Building, Room 3614
26 Federal Plaza
New York, NY 10278
(212) 264-0300

REGION 3: NEW YORK
Federal Building, Room 901
111 West Huron Street
Buffalo, NY 14202
(716) 846-4931

Federal Building, Room 342
Clinton Avenue at
North Pearl Street
Albany, NY 12207
(518) 472-2215

REGION 4: DELAWARE, NEW JERSEY, PENNSYLVANIA
One Independence Mall,
7th Floor
615 Chestnut Street
Philadelphia, PA 19106
(215) 597-7601

REGION 5: DELAWARE, D.C., MARYLAND, PENNSYLVANIA, VIRGINIA, WEST VIRGINIA
Candler Building, 4th Floor
109 Market Place
Baltimore, MD 21202
(410) 962-2822

REGION 6: PENNSYLVANIA, WEST VIRGINIA
Federal Building, Room 1501
1000 Liberty Avenue
Pittsburgh, PA 15222
(412) 644-2977

REGION 7: MICHIGAN
Federal Building, Room 300
477 Michigan Avenue
Detroit, MI 48226
(313) 226-3200

REGION 8: OHIO
Federal Building, Suite 1695
1240 East Ninth Street
Cleveland, OH 44199
(216) 522-3715

REGION 9: INDIANA, KENTUCKY, OHIO, WEST VIRGINIA
Federal Building, Room 3003
550 Main Street
Cincinnati, OH 45202
(513) 684-3686

REGION 10: AL, GEORGIA, TENNESSEE
Marietta Tower, Suite 2400101
Marietta Street, NW
Atlanta, GA 30323
(404) 331-2896

2025 Third Avenue North
Birmingham, AL 352203
(205) 731-1062

REGION 11: NORTH CAROLINA, SOUTH CAROLINA, TENNESSEE, VIRGINIA, WEST VIRGINIA
U.S. Courthouse and
Federal Building, Room 447
215 North Main Street
Winston-Salem, NC 27101

REGION 12: FLORIDA, GEORGIA
201 East Kennedy Boulevard
Tampa, FL 33602
(813) 228-2641

Federal Building, Room 916
51 Southwest First Avenue
Miami, FL 33130
(305) 350-5391

Federal Building, Room 278
400 West Bay Street
Jacksonville, FL 32202
(904) 791-3768

REGION 13: ILLINOIS, INDIANA
200 West Adams Street
Chicago, IL 60606
(312) 353-7570

REGION 14: ILLINOIS, MISSOURI
611 North 10th Street,
Room 400
St. Louis, MO 63101
(314) 425-4167

REGION 15: AL, FLORIDA, LOUISIANA, MISSISSIPPI
1515 Poydras Street,
Room 610
New Orleans, LA 70112
(504) 589-6361

REGION 16: ARKANSAS, TEXAS
Federal Office Building,
Room 8-A-24
819 Taylor Street
Fort Worth, TX 76102
(817) 334-2921

440 Louisiana Street,
Suite 550
Houston, TX 77002
(713) 220-2365

REGION 17: IOWA, KANSAS, MISSOURI, NEBRASKA
5799 Broadmoor, Suite 500
Mission, KS 66202
(913) 236-2777

Cranston Building, Suite 900
111 W. 5th Street
Tulsa, OK 74101

REGION 18: IOWA, MINNESOTA, NORTH DAKOTA, SOUTH DAKOTA, WISCONSIN
Federal Building, Room 316
110 South 4th Street
Minneapolis, MN 55401
(612) 348-1757

210 Walnut Street, Room 909
Des Moines, IA 50309
(515) 284-4391

REGION 19: ALASKA, IDAHO, MONTANA, OREGON, WASHINGTON
Federal Building, Room 2948
915 Second Avenue
Seattle, WA 98174
(206) 553-4532

Federal Office Building
Room 21
222 West Seventh Avenue
Anchorage, AK 99513
(907) 271-5015

222 S.W. Columbia
Portland, OR 97201
(503) 326-3085

REGION 20: CALIFORNIA, HAWAII
901 Market Street
San Francisco, CA 94103
(415) 744-6810

300 Ala Moana Boulevard
Room 7318
Honolulu, HI 96850
(808) 541-2814

REGION 21: CALIFORNIA
811 Wilshire Boulevard
Los Angeles, CA 90017
(213) 894-5200

555 West Beach Street
Suite 302
San Diego, CA 92101
(619) 293-6184

REGION 22: NEW JERSEY
Federal Building, Room 1600
970 Broad Street
Newark, NJ 07102
(201) 645-2100

REGION 24: PUERTO RICO, U.S. VIRGIN ISLANDS
Federal Building, Room 591
150 Avenue Carlos E. Chardon
Room 591
Hato Rey, PR 00918
(809) 766-5347

REGION 25: INDIANA, KENTUCKY
Federal Office Building
Room 238
575 North Pennsylvania St.
Indianapolis, IN 46204
(317) 226-7430

REGION 26: ARKANSAS, MISSISSIPPI, TENNESSEE
Mid-Memphis Tower Building
Suite 800
1407 Union Avenue
P.O. Box 41599
Memphis, TN 38104
(901) 521-2725

Federal Building
801 Broadway
Nashville, TN 37203
(615) 736-592

303 W. Capital, Room 350
Little Rock, AR 72201
(501) 378-6311

REGION 27: COLORADO, IDAHO, MONTANA, NEBRASKA, WYOMING
600 17th Street
Denver, CO 80202
(303) 844-3551

REGION 28: ARIZONA, NEW MEXICO, NEVADA, TEXAS
234 North Central Avenue
Suite 440
Phoenix, AZ 85004
(602) 241-2350

505 Marquette Avenue NW
Suite 1820
Albuquerque, NM 87102

U.S. Post Office &
Courthouse Bldg.
Room 565
615 E. Houston Street
San Antonio, TX 78205
(915) 534-6434

600 Las Vegas Blvd., South
Suite 400
Las Vegas, NV 89101

REGION 29: NEW YORK
75 Clinton Street, 4th Floor
Brooklyn, NY 11201
(718) 330-7713

REGION 30: MICHIGAN, WISCONSIN
310 West Wisconsin Avenue
Suite 700
Milwaukee, WI 53203
(414) 297-3861

REGION 31: CALIFORNIA
Federal Building, Room 12100
11000 Wilshire Avenue
Los Angeles, CA 90024
(310) 575-7352

REGION 32: CALIFORNIA, NEVADA
Breuner Building, 2nd Floor
2201 Broadway
P.O. Box 12983
Oakland, CA 94612
(415) 273-7200

REGION 33: ILLINOIS, IOWA
Savings Center Tower, 16th Fl.
411 Hamilton Blvd.
Peoria, IL 61602
(309) 671-7080

REGION 34: CONNECTICUT
One Commercial Plaza
Hartford, CT 06103
(203) 240-3522

National Headquarters
1099 14th Street, N.W.
Washington, DC 20570
(202) 273-10003

OCCUPATIONAL SAFETY AND HEALTH ADMINISTRATION (OSHA)

OSHA has 85 area offices throughout the county which handle safety complaints. To find the area office nearest you, call one of the Regional Offices listed below.

REGION I: CONNECTICUT, MAINE, NEW HAMPSHIRE, RHODE ISLAND, VERMONT
133 Portland Street, 1st Floor
Boston, MA 02114
(617) 565-7164

REGION II: NEW JERSEY, NEW YORK, PUERTO RICO, VIRGIN ISLANDS
201 Varick Street, Room 670
New York, NY 10014
(212) 337-2378

REGION III: DISTRICT OF COLUMBIA, DELAWARE, MARYLAND, PENNSYLVANIA, VIRGINIA, WEST VIRGINIA
Gateway Building, Suite 2100
3535 Market Street
Philadelphia, PA 19104
(215) 596-1201

REGION IV: AL, FLORIDA, GEORGIA, KENTUCKY, MISSISSIPPI, NORTH CAROLINA, SOUTH CAROLINA, TENNESSEE
1375 Peachtree Street, NE
Suite 587
Atlanta, GA 30367
(404) 347-3573

REGION V: ILLINOIS, INDIANA, MICHIGAN, MINNESOTA, OHIO, WISCONSIN
230 South Dearborn Street
Room 3244
Chicago, IL 60604
(312) 353-2220

REGION VI: ARKANSAS, LOUISIANA, NEW MEXICO, OKLAHOMA, TEXAS
525 Griffin Street, Room 602
Dallas, TX 75202
(214) 767-4731

REGION VII: IOWA, KANSAS, MISSOURI, NEBRASKA
City Center Square
1100 Main Street, Suite 800
Kansas City, MO 64105
(816) 426-5861

REGION VIII: COLORADO, MONTANA, NORTH DAKOTA, SOUTH DAKOTA, UTAH, WYOMING
Suite 1690
1999 Broadway
Denver, CO 8000202
(303) 391-5858

REGION IX: AMERICAN SAMOA, ARIZONA, CALIFORNIA, GUAM, HAWAII, NEVADA
71 Stevenson Street, Room 420
San Francisco, CA 94105
(415) 744-6670

REGION X: ALASKA, IDAHO, OREGON, WASHINGTON
111 Third Avenue Suite 715
Seattle, WA 98101-3212
(206) 553-5930

U.S. DEPARTMENT OF LABOR (DOL)– WAGE AND HOUR DIVISION

The Employment and Training administration is an agency within the Department of Labor (DOL) which funds and regulates training and employment programs administered by state and local agencies and federal workers' compensation laws (the Federal Employees' Compensation Act, the Longshoremen's & Harbor Workers' Compensation Act of 1927, and the Black Lung Benefits Reform Act of 1977). This agency also encompasses the offices of the Wage & Hour Division and Federal Contract Compliance Programs. The Wage and Hour Division has 75 district offices throughout the country which handle overtime and minimum wage complaints. To locate the district office nearest you, call the Regional office.

REGION 1: CONNECTICUT, MAINE, MASSACHUSETTS, NEW HAMPSHIRE, RHODE ISLAND, VERMONT
Employment Standards Administration
John F. Kennedy Federal Bldg.
Room 1612C
Boston, MA 02203
(617) 565-2066

REGION 2: NEW JERSEY, NEW YORK, PUERTO RICO, VIRGIN ISLANDS
Employment Standards Administration
201 Varick St.
New York, NY 10014
(212) 337-2000

REGION 3: DISTRICT OF COLUMBIA, DELAWARE, MARYLAND, PENNSYLVANIA, VIRGINIA, WEST VIRGINIA
Employment Standards Administration
Gateway Bldg., Room 15230
3535 Market Street
Philadelphia, PA 19104
(215) 596-1185

REGION 4: ALABAMA, FLORIDA, GEORGIA, KENTUCKY, MISSISSIPPI, NORTH CAROLINA, SOUTH CAROLINA, TENNESSEE
Employment Standards Administration
1375 Peachtree St. N.E. Room 662
Atlanta, GA 30367
(404) 347-4801

REGION 5: ILLINOIS, INDIANA, MICHIGAN, OHIO, WISCONSIN
Employment Standards Administration
230 South Dearborn St.
8th Floor
Chicago, IL 60604
(312) 353-7280

REGION 6: ARKANSAS, LOUISIANA, NEW MEXICO, OKLAHOMA, TEXAS
Employment Standards
Administration
525 Griffin Square Bldg.
Room 800
Young & Griffin Streets
Dallas, TX 75202
(214) 767-4771

REGION 7: IOWA, KANSAS, NEBRASKA, MISSOURI
Employment Standards
Administration
Federal Office Building
Room 2000
911 Walnut Street
Kansas City, MO 64106
(816) 426-5381

REGION 8: COLORADO, MONTANA, NORTH DAKOTA, SOUTH DAKOTA, UTAH, WYOMING
Employment Standards
Administration
1801 California Street
Suite 930
Denver, CO 80202
(303) 391-6780

REGION 9: CALIFORNIA, ARIZONA, HAWAII, NEVADA
Employment Standards
Administration
71 Stevenson Street
Room 930
San Francisco, CA 94105
(415) 744-6625

REGION 10: WASHINGTON, OREGON, IDAHO, ALASKA
Employment Standards
Administration
1111 Third Avenue, Suite 600
Seattle, WA 98101
(206) 553-1914

FEDERAL SOURCES OF PENSION RIGHTS INFORMATION

U.S. DEPARTMENT OF LABOR DIVISION OF PUBLIC AFFAIRS PENSION AND WELFARE BENEFIT ADMINISTRATION
200 Constitution Avenue,
N.W., Room N-5656
Washington, DC 20210
(202) 219-8233

or

CONSUMER INFORMATION CENTER
Dept. 365-B
Pueblo, CO 81009
(write for publications list)

PENSION BENEFIT GUARANTY CORPORATION
1200 K Street, N.W.
Washington, DC 20005
(202) 326-4040

INTERNAL REVENUE SERVICE
(800) 829-3676

RAILROAD RETIREMENT BOARD
844 Rush Street
Chicago, IL 60611
(312) 751-4500

SOCIAL SECURITY ADMINISTRATION
6401 Security Boulevard
Baltimore, MD 212351
(800) 772-1213

OFFICE OF PERSONNEL MANAGEMENT RETIREMENT OPERATIONS CENTER
P.O. Box 45
Boyers, PA 16017
(412) 794-8442 or
(412) 794-8690

DEPARTMENT OF VETERANS AFFAIRS
1120 Vermont Avenue NW
Washington, DC 20421
(202) 418-4343

U.S. GOVERNMENT PRINTING OFFICE SUPERINTENDENT OF DOCUMENTS
732 N. Capitol Street NW
Washington, DC 20401
(202) 512-1800

Appendix C—Non-Governmental Resources

Employment Law

The National Employment Lawyers Association
535 Pacific Avenue
San Francisco, CA 94133
(415) 397-6335

General Legal Aid and Defender Association
1625 K Street N.W., 8th Floor
Washington, DC 20006
(202) 452-0620

Legal Services Corporation
750 1st Street N.E.
Washington, DC 20002
(202) 336-8800

Southern Poverty Law Center
400 Washington Ave
Montgomery, AL 36104
(205) 264-0286

Civil Rights In General (Including Discrimination)

American Civil Liberties Union (ACLU)
132 West 43rd Street
New York, NY 10036
(212) 944-9800

Center for Constitutional Rights
666 Broadway
New York, NY 10012
(212) 614-6464

Center for Law and Social Policy
1751 N Street, NW
Washington, DC 20036
(202) 328-5140

Lawyers Committee for Civil Rights Under Law
1400 I Street, NW, Suite 400
Washington, DC 20005
(202) 371-1212

National Lawyers Guild
55 Avenue of the Americas
New York, NY 10013
(212) 996-5000

Rights of Racial, Ethnic, or Other Groups

Asian-American Legal Defense and Education Fund
99 Hudson Street, 12th Floor
New York, NY 10013
(212) 966-5932

Mexican-American Legal Defense and Education Fund
182 2nd Street, 2nd Floor
San Francisco, CA 94105
(415) 543-5598

National Association for the Advancement of Colored People (NAACP)
4805 Mount Hope Drive
Baltimore, MD 21215
(414) 358-8900

National Urban League (specializes in race discrimination)
500 East 62nd Street
New York, NY 10021
(212) 310-9000

NAACP Legal Defense Fund
99 Hudson Street, Suite 1600
New York, NY 10013
(212) 219-1900

National Conference of Black Lawyers
129 West 119th Street
New York, NY 10026
(212) 864-4000

National Veterans Legal Services Project
2001 S Street, NW, Suite 610
Washington, DC 200
(202) 265-8305

Puerto Rican Legal Defense and Education Fund
99 Hudson Street
New York, NY 10013
(212) 219-3360

Native American Rights Fund
1506 Broadway
Boulder, CO 80302
(303) 447-8760

American Association for Retired Persons (AARP) Legal Advocacy Group Litigation
601 E Street, N.W.
Washington, DC 20049
(202) 434-2060

Lambda Legal Defense and Education Fund
666 Broadway, 12th Floor
New York, NY 10012
(212) 995-8585

President's Committee On Employment of People and Disabilities
1331 F. Street, N.W.
Washington, DC 20004
(202) 376-6200

JOB ACCOMMODATION NETWORK

WEST VIRGINIA UNIVERSITY
918 Chestnut Ridge Road
Suite 1
P.O. Box 6080
Morgantown, WV 26506-6080
(800) 232-9675

NATIONAL ASSOCIATION OF PROTECTION AND ADVOCACY SYSTEMS
900 Second Street, N.E.
Suite 211
Washington, DC 20002
(202) 408-9514

SEX DISCRIMINATION, SEXUAL HARASSMENT, AND WOMEN'S ISSUES

9 TO 5, NATIONAL ASSOCIATION OF WORKING WOMEN
614 Superior Avenue
Cleveland, OH 44113
(216) 566-9308
(800) 522-0925 (hotline)

U.S. DEPARTMENT OF LABOR WOMEN'S BUREAU
200 Constitutional Ave, NW
Washington, DC 20210
(202) 219-8913

NOW LEGAL DEFENSE AND EDUCATION FUND
99 Hudson Street, 12th Floor
New York, NY 10013
(212) 925-6635

WOMEN'S LEGAL DEFENSE FUND
Suite 7101
875 Connecticut Ave, NW
Washington, DC 20009
(202) 986-2600

U.S. DEPARTMENT OF LABOR, WOMEN'S BUREAU
200 Constitution Avenue, NW
Washington, DC 20210
(800) 827-5355

RIGHTS OF UNION MEMBERS

AMERICAN FEDERATION OF LABOR AND CONGRESS OF INDUSTRIAL ORGANIZATIONS (AFL-CIO)
815-16th Street, N.W.
Washington, DC 20006
(202) 637-5000

ASSOCIATION FOR UNION DEMOCRACY
500 State Street
Brooklyn, NY 11217
(718) 855-6650

PENSION INFORMATION

AMERICAN ASSOCIATION OF RETIRED PERSONS
601 E Street, N.W.
Washington, DC 20049
(202) 434-2277

NATIONAL SENIOR CITIZENS LAW CENTER
1815 H Street, N.W., Suite 700
Washington, DC 20006
(202) 887-5280

OLDER WOMEN'S LEAGUE
666 11th Street, N.W., Suite 700
Washington, DC 20001
(202) 783-6686

PENSION RIGHTS CENTER
918 16th Street, N.W., Suite 704
Washington, DC 20006
(202) 296-3776

NATIONAL COUNCIL OF SENIOR CITIZENS
8403 Colesville Road
Suite 1200
Silver Springs, MD 20910
(301) 578-8999

PENSION EDUCATION CLEARINGHOUSE
P.O. Box 19821
Washington, DC 20036

NATIONAL ALLIANCE OF SENIOR CITIZENS
1744 Riggs Place, N.W.
Washington, DC 20006
(202) 986-0117

GENERAL INFORMATION FOR EMPLOYEES

NATIONAL EMPLOYEE RIGHTS INSTITUTE
414 Walnut Street, Suite 911
Cincinnati, OH 45202
(800) HOW-NERI

WORKING TODAY
Times Square Post Office
P.O. Box 681
New York, NY 10108
(212) 840-6066

EMPLOYMENT LAW CENTER
1663 Mission, Suite 400
San Francisco, CA 94103
(415) 864-8848

LANGUAGE RIGHTS LINE,
(800) 864-1664, provides advice and referrals to persons subjected to language based discrimination.

WORK AND FAMILY LINE,
(800) 880-8047, provides advice and referral services to those whose Family and Medical Leave Act rights have been violated.

DISGRUNTLED, THE BUSINESS MAGAZINE FOR PEOPLE WHO WORK FOR A LIVING
http://www.disgruntled.com
e-mail-dslevine@disgruntled.com

NATIONAL EMPLOYMENT LAW PROJECT
55 John Street
New York, NY 10038
(212) 285-3025

Appendix D—Sample Letters of Appeal

Example 1:
Professional/Management Level Downsized Employee

Mary T. Lesser
Marketing Analyst
222 Second Street
Second City, Illinois 55555
January 1, 1997

Mr. Barry Berry
Vice President of Operations
New Wave Surf Boards
First City, Illinois 55556

Dear Mr. Berry:

As you are aware, New Wave Surf Boards has recently undergone divisional restructuring. Part of this restructuring included elimination of my position from marketing.

I was informed that the reason my position was chosen for elimination was that my area of specialty, the East Coast market, was not essential to the company's continued growth.

I believe that before my termination is final, my contributions to the marketing department should be reviewed. I have developed unique contacts in the East Coast market, but have never been given the opportunity to develop other markets or new strategies for existing markets. My last appraisal indicated that the company was aware of and appreciated my creativity, innovation, and hard work. I have consistently shown good results in the difficult East Coast market.

I would like the opportunity to discuss my selection for termination. I believe that I have unique skills that will increase New Wave Surf Board's market share, which I know is of utmost importance to the company.

Thank you for taking the time to read and consider my request. I will contact you next week to set up a convenient time for us to meet. If you have any questions, please call me.

Sincerely,

Mary T. Lesser

Example 2:
Terminated or Downsized For Alleged Poor Performance

Pat Smith
Media Director
1111 First Street
Walnut City, Nevada 55555
January 1, 1997

Ms. Martha Kraft
Manager
Bells & Whistles Section
Hoopla Corporation
999 Ninth Street
Hazelnut City, Nevada 55554

Dear Ms. Kraft:

Thank you for taking the time to read and consider my letter. As you may know, I have been notified that my employment with Hoopla Corporation will end as of January 3, 1997. I was told that the reason for this decision was poor performance on my part.

I believe that a mistake has been made in my case. I have worked for this company for eight years and consistently received good performance evaluations, until a new supervisor was hired this past year. Mr. Groves has been my supervisor for only six months and has had little opportunity to see my work firsthand. He never warned me that he thought my performance was substandard. I understand that Mr. Groves' nephew, Rick, is to take my position when I am gone.

I do not believe that I have been given an adequate opportunity to demonstrate or discuss my skills with Mr. Groves. I also believe that my termination is unfair since I never received any indication that my performance was poor.

I would like the opportunity to discuss my situation with you. Please let me know when you are available.

Sincerely,

Pat Smith

EXAMPLE 3:
USING HANDBOOK APPEALS PROCEDURE

Jay Washington
Printer
3333 Third Street
Nevermore, Maryland 55557
January 1, 1997

Kathleen Brooks
Supervisor
Machine Machinery
5555 Fifth Street
Nevermore, Maryland 55558

Dear Ms. Brooks:

I was recently notified that my employment with Machine Machinery will be ending as of February 1, 1997. Our company handbook states that I have the right to challenge termination, and I would like to take advantage of this right to discuss with you the reasons that Machine Machinery should retain me in its employ.

According to the handbook, the first step is a meeting between the employee and his supervisor. Therefore, I request that we meet as soon as possible. I am available any afternoon or evening this week.

I look forward to hearing from you.

Sincerely,

Jay Washington

EXAMPLE 1:
MODEST REFERRAL

(Company Letterhead)

To.
[Either fill in company name here or make letter "to whom it may concern"]

Re: Willanda Employee

Ms. Employee worked for our company for over ten years. Recently, we have had to cut back our workforce due to economic conditions. Unfortunately, Ms. Employee lost her position with our company as a result of this restructuring. Ms. Employee is knowledgeable of payroll and accounting functions and has proven computer skills. She is also punctual and courteous.

While our company policy precludes us from giving recommendations for employees, Ms. Employee has been given permission to attach her most recent performance evaluations to this letter. Additionally, you may, if you wish, contact her most recent supervisor, Thomas Thomas, for more information about her work at our company.

Sincerely,

[the highest level company official obtainable]

EXAMPLE 2:
IDEAL REFERENCE

(Company Letterhead)

To.
[Either fill in company name here or make letter "to whom it may concern"]

Re: Willanda Employee

Ms. Willanda Employee was employed by our company for over ten years. Due to economic conditions, our company has had to reduce its workforce. One unfortunate result of this downsizing is the loss of Ms. Employee's services.

Ms. Employee has consistently been an outstanding performer in our payroll and accounting department. She has in-depth knowledge of accounting principles and an admirable attention to detail. She has had significant experience with the following computer applications: [list here]. She is a creative problem solver and has "saved" the payroll for us on a number of occasions.

Ms. Employee is a punctual, courteous, and conscientious worker. If you have any questions, please contact her most recent supervisor, Thomas Thomas. Her outstanding performance evaluations are attached to this letter.

Our company made the decision to outsource our accounting and payroll functions, resulting in the loss of Ms. Employee's position. We will miss her professional demeanor and teamwork.

Sincerely,

[highest level company official obtainable]

CHARGE OF DISCRIMINATION	AGENCY	CHARGE NUMBER
This form is affected by the Privacy Act of 1974; See Privacy Act Statement before completing this form.	☐ FEPA ☒ EEOC	

_____ and EEOC

State or local Agency, if any

NAME *(Indicate Mr., Ms., Mrs.)*	HOME TELEPHONE *(Include Area Code)*

STREET ADDRESS	CITY, STATE AND ZIP CODE	DATE OF BIRTH / /

NAMED IS THE EMPLOYER, LABOR ORGANIZATION, EMPLOYMENT AGENCY APPRENTICESHIP COMMITTEE, STATE OR LOCAL GOVERNMENT AGENCY WHO DISCRIMINATED AGAINST ME *(If more than one list below.)*

NAME	NUMBER OF EMPLOYEES, MEMBERS	TELEPHONE *(Include Area Code)*

STREET ADDRESS	CITY, STATE AND ZIP CODE	COUNTY

NAME	TELEPHONE NUMBER *(Include Area Code)*

STREET ADDRESS	CITY, STATE AND ZIP CODE	COUNTY

CAUSE OF DISCRIMINATION BASED ON *(Check appropriate box(es))*

☐ RACE ☐ COLOR ☐ SEX ☐ RELIGION ☐ NATIONAL ORIGIN ☐ RETALIATION ☐ AGE ☐ DISABILITY ☐ OTHER *(Specify)*

DATE DISCRIMINATION TOOK PLACE
EARLIEST *(ADEA/EPA)*   LATEST *(ALL)*
/ / -   / /
☐ CONTINUING ACTION

THE PARTICULARS ARE *(If additional space is needed, attach extra sheet(s)):*

☐ I also want this charge filed with the EEOC. I will advise the agencies if I change my address or telephone number and I will cooperate fully with them in the processing of my charge in accordance with their procedures.	NOTARY - *(When necessary for State and Local Requirements)*
I declare under penalty of perjury that the foregoing is true and correct.	I swear or affirm that I have read the above charge and that it is true to the best of my knowledge, information and belief.
	SIGNATURE OF COMPLAINANT
	SUBSCRIBED AND SWORN TO BEFORE ME THIS DATE *(Day, month, and year)*
Date Charging Party *(Signature)*	

EEOC TEST FORM 5 (09/01/91)

INDEX

401(k) plan, 32, 35

ACLU. *See* American Civil Liberties Union
ADA. *See* Americans with Disabilities Act
ADEA. *See* Age Discrimination in Employment Act
Administrative remedies, 110-15
Adverse action, 90-91, 93
Age, discrimination based on, 90, 98, 100, 110
Age Discrimination in Employment Act (ADEA), 69-70, 95, 111, 136
Agreement
    consulting, 43
    non-compete, 25-26
    non-disparagement, 41
    settlement, 24, 26-27
    See also Contract
Alcohol
    addiction, 70
    avoiding, 131
Alternative dispute resolution, 120-22
American Association of Retired Persons (AARP), 105, 142-43
American Civil Liberties Union (ACLU), 105, 142
American Federation of Labor and Congress of Industrial Organizations (AFL-CIO), 143
Americans with Disabilities Act (ADA), 70-71, 95, 100, 111, 136
Anatomy of an Illness, 133
Anger, 27, 129, 132
Answer (to complaint), 117
Anti-retaliation provisions, 73
Anti-trust laws
    federal, 78
    official citations to, 136
Appeals, 119
Arbitration, 121

Asian-American Legal Defense and Education Fund, 142
Assault and battery, 85-86, 99
Association for Union Democracy, 143
Attendance record, 102
Attorney
    contract for services with, 107-08
    fees for, 107-08
    finding experienced, 104-05
    initial consultation with, 106
    negotiation by, 37
    release letter review by, 24
    when to contact, 104-09
    working with, 106-09
Attorney-client relationship, 108-09

Back pay, 22, 119-20
Bankruptcy Act, 78, 136
Bar association, 105
Bargaining power, 22, 40
Battery. *See* Assault and battery
Behavior, 27
Bias
    as circumstantial evidence, 89
    toward protected class, 91
Black listing, 82
Black Lung Benefits Reform Act of 1977, 140
Blue-collar employees, 42
Boards of Adjustment, 76
Bonus plans, 75
Bureau of Employee Services, 45

Case. *See* Court case; Lawsuit
CBA. *See* Collective bargaining agreement
Center for Constitutional Rights, 142
Center for Law and Social Policy, 142

Chain of command
    appeal to, 23
    negotiating up, 38
Child, birth or adoption of, 72
Circumstantial evidence, 89-91
Civil rights
    non-government resources, 142
    state agency for, 99
Civil Rights Act, 95
    of 1964, 67-69, 136
    of 1991, 67
    other, 77
Civil service
    employees, 58-59. *See also* Government employees
    job registries, 126
Civil Service Reform Act, 79
Claims
    contract, 99
    discrimination, 89-92, 98, 110-15
    ERISA, 94-95
    future, 25
    investigating by the Department of Labor, 113-14
    other employees with same type, 104
    pension or retirement, 25
    public policy, 87
    release of, 24-25, 30
    retaliation, 92-94, 110-15
    state law, 115
    tort, 99
    union activities, 113
    unsafe working conditions, 114-15
    workers compensation, 25, 87
Clayton Act, 136
COBRA, 52-54
Collective bargaining agreement (CBA), 57-58, 66, 100-01, 112-13, 121
Color, discrimination based on, 67-68, 98, 110
Commission, 80

Common law, 82
Company bulletins, 102
Competitive service, 59
Complaint, 117
Complaint process, 16
Confidentiality agreement, 20
Confidentiality requirements, 26-27
Consideration, 61
Consolidated Omnibus Budget and Reconciliation Act (COBRA), 52-54
Constructive discharge, 23
Consulting agreement, 43
Consumer Credit Protection Act, 76, 100, 113, 135-36
Consumer Information Center, 141
Contingency fee, 107
Contract
    for attorney's services, 107-08
    breach of, 61, 83, 99
    claims, state laws for, 99
    employment, 61
    implied, 63
    legally enforceable, 61
    oral, 63
    union, violations of, 112-13
    what is? 61-63
    written, 62
    See also Agreement
Counseling
    precomplaint federal employee, 112
    professional, 132-33
Court case
    building your, 102
    common characteristics and processes for, 116-22
    filing "pro se," 116
    See also Lawsuit
Cousins, Norman, 133
Covenant of good faith and fair dealing, 64
Crime, refusal to commit, 87

Damages, 119-20
Defamation, 83-84, 99, 120

Defendant, 117
Defined benefit plans, 33
Defined contribution plans, 33
Demotion, as adverse action, 90
Department of Labor. See U.S. Department of Labor
Department of Veterans Affairs. See U.S. Department of Veterans Affairs
Deposition, 107-08, 117
Detrimental reliance, 64
Direct evidence, 89
Disability
    discrimination based on, 90, 98, 100, 110
    insurance, 54
Discharge. See Termination
Disciplinary warnings, 102
Discovery, 117-18
Discrimination, 89-95
    based on
        age, 90, 98, 100, 110
        color, 67-68, 98, 110
        disability, 90, 98, 100, 110
        family/marital status, 98
        gender, 67-68, 98, 100
        national origin, 67-68, 98, 100, 110
        pension plan status, 94-95
        pregnancy, 110
        qualifications, 90
        race, 67-68, 98, 100, 110
        religion, 69, 100, 110
        retaliation, 100
        salary and wage, 79
        sexual orientation, 98
    charge of, 111
    claims. See Discrimination claims
    evidence of, 89-92
    intolerable situation due to, 22
    laws forbidding, 57
    physical harassment and, 86
    "prima facie case" of, 90
    protesting perceived, 92-93
    resignation due to, 21
    state laws on, 82
    Title VII and, 67

Discrimination claims
    administrative remedies for, 110-15
    for federal employers, 112
    filing with EEOC for, 110-12
    state laws for, 98-99
Disparate impact, 68
Disparate treatment, 68
Documents
    confidential, 20
    gathering for court case, 102
    to protest termination, 20
    release, 24
    requests for employer's, 117
    settlement, 24
Downsizing, 13, 38
Drugs
    addiction to, 70
    avoiding, 131
    testing for, 85
Due process, 58

Early retirement, 33, 42-43
EEOC. See Equal Employment Opportunity Commission
Emotional and mental distress, 120
Employee
    bargaining power of, 40
    federal, 79
    government, 58-59
    leased, 60
    non-governmental information sources for, 143
    as Plaintiff, 117
    private sector, 56-57
    right of union membership, 66
    with same type claim, 104
    temporary employment agency, 60
    union. See Union employee
Employee Assistance Program (EAP), 133
Employee Polygraph Protection Act (EPA), 74-75, 100, 113, 136

Employee Retirement Income and Security Act of 1974 (ERISA), 34, 75, 93-95, 101, 136
Employee Rights Clearinghouse, 5
Employee Rights and Employment Policy Journal, 5
Employer
    adverse action by, 93
    contesting unemployment compensation, 46-47
    countering denials of, 91-92, 94
    as Defendant, 117
    financial responsibility for wages, 36
    grievance or complaint process of, 16
    grossly unreasonable, 37
    joint, 60
    knowledge of protected conduct, 93
    legal relationship to, 55-64
    personnel files of, 20-21
    prospective, 23
    public policy violation by, 87-88
    reasons for negotiating severance, 41
    severance pay policy of, 30
    termination policies of, 15, 62
    trade secrets of, 26-27
Employment
    coping with loss of, 14
    terms of, 55-64
Employment-at-will doctrine, 56
Employment contract, 61
Employment law, 65-95
    non-governmental resources for, 142
    right to sue for violation of, 37
Employment Law Center, 143
Employment relationship
    ending, 20-28
    interference with, 88
    state laws affecting, 82

Employment and Training Administration, 140
Enforceable promise, 63-64
Engagement fee, 107
EPA. See Employee Polygraph Protection Act
Equal Employment Opportunity Commission (EEOC), 22, 100, 135
    attitude toward arbitration, 121
    filing claims with, 110-12
    local offices, 137
    time limits for filing with, 101
    sample charge form, 149
Equal Pay Act, 36, 66, 79-80, 136
ERISA. See Employee Retirement Income Security Act of 1974
Events, record of, 28
Evidence
    circumstantial, 89-91
    direct, 89
    of discrimination, 89-92
    that protected conduct led to termination, 93-94
Excepted service, 59
Executives, separation packages of, 41
Exercise, 131
Expenses
    out-of-pocket, 107-08
    trial, 119

Fair Labor Standards Act (FSLA), 36, 60, 80-81, 100, 113-14, 135-36
False Claims Act, 77, 95, 100, 136
False imprisonment, 86-87, 99
Family, COBRA coverage for, 53-54
Family/marital status, 98
Family and Medical Leave Act (FMLA), 72, 93, 95, 100, 113, 135
Federal Contract Compliance Programs, 140

Federal employees, 112. See also Government employees
Federal Employees' Compensation Act, 140
Federal governmental offices, 135, 137-41. See also names of specific offices
Federal Law Anti-Retaliation Provisions, 95
Federal laws
    Age Discrimination in Employment Act (ADEA), 69-70, 95, 111, 136
    Americans with Disabilities Act (ADA), 70-71, 95, 100, 111, 136
    Anti-retaliation provisions of, 73
    Anti-trust laws, 78, 136
    Bankruptcy Act, 78, 136
    Civil Rights Acts, 95
    of 1964, 67-69, 136
    of 1991, 67
    other, 77
    Civil Service Reform Act, 79
    Consumer Credit Protection Act, 76, 100, 113, 135-36
    Employee Polygraph Protection Act (EPA), 74-75, 100, 113, 136
    Employee Retirement Income and Security Act (ERISA), 34, 75, 93-95, 101, 136
    Equal Pay Act, 36, 66, 79-80, 136
    Fair Labor Standards Act (FSLA), 80-81, 100, 113-14, 135-36
    False Claims Act, 77, 95, 100, 136
    Family and Medical Leave Act (FMLA), 72, 93, 95, 100, 113, 135
    Immigration and Naturalization Act, 78
    Juror Credit Protection Act, 76

Juror Protection Act, 100, 136

National Labor Relations Act (NLRA), 66-67, 136

official citations to, 136

persons protected by, 95

protecting private sector employees, 56-57

Racketeer Influenced and Corrupt Organizations Act (RICO), 76, 100, 136

Railway Labor Act (RLA), 76, 136

Uniformed Services Employment and Reemployment Rights Act of 1994, 76, 100, 136

wage, 36

Whistleblower Protection Act, 78, 136

Worker Adjustment Retraining and Notification Act (WARN), 73-74, 100-01, 136

Finances, post-termination, 29-54, 130

Firing

as adverse action, 90

for gross misconduct, COBRA and, 53

obtaining reason in writing, 21

See also Termination

FMLA. *See* Family and Medical Leave Act

Fraud, 76, 85, 99

Freedom of Information Act, 111

Fringe benefits, 31-32

Front pay, 120

FSLA. *See* Fair Labor Standards Act

Garnishment of wages, 76

Gender

discrimination based on, 110

See also Sex

General Legal Aid and Defender Association, 142

Governmental offices

Department of Labor (DOL), 140-41

Occupational Safety & Health Administration (OSHA), 139-40

for pension rights information sources, 141

See also names of specific offices

Government employee, 58-59. *See also* Federal employees

Grievance procedure, 16, 22

union, 57

for union employees, 17

Gross misconduct, 53

Handbooks, employer, 102

Harassment

for religious affiliation, 69

resignation due to, 21

sexual, 73, 76, 143

unemployment compensation and, 47

Health insurance, 52-54, 133

Health Insurance Portability and Accounting Act, 54

Hourly employees, 42

Immigration and Naturalization Act, 78

Implied contract, 63

Independent contractor, 59-60

Individual benefit statement, 32

Individual Retirement Account (IRA), 35

Insurance

disability, 54

health, 52-54, 133

Intentional infliction of emotional distress, 83, 99

Interference with contract rights, 99

Internal appeal process, 23

Internal Revenue Code, 60

Internal Revenue Service, 141

Internet, as job lead source, 124, 126

Interrogatories, 117

Invasion of privacy, 84-85, 99

Job

applications and interviews for, 127-28

coping with loss of, 14, 129-33

saving your, 15-17

security, 62

strategies for finding, 124-28

See also Employment

Job Accommodation Network, 143

Joint employer, 60

Journal, 103, 132

Juror Credit Protection Act, 76

Juror Protection Act, 100, 136

Jury duty, 87

Just cause termination, unemployment compensation and, 46

Labor unions. *See* Unions

Lambda Legal Defense and Education Fund, 142

Language Rights Line, 143

Laws

common, 82

federal. *See* Federal laws

state. *See* State laws

Lawsuit

appeals to, 119

attorney filing, 104

downside of, 134

EEOC filing, 111

frivolous, 120

proceeds from, 124

See also Court case

Lawyer

court case without, 116

See also Attorney

Lawyers Committee for Civil Rights Under Law, 142

Layoffs

in past, 13

severance package and mass, 38

temporary, 74

Leased employees, 60

Legal Aid Society, 105

Legal aliens, 78

Legal process, 117

Legal Services Corporation, 142

Lerner, Helen, 132

Letter
    of appeal, 27
        professional/manage-
        ment level downsized
        employee, 144
        terminated or downsized
        for alleged poor per-
        formance, 145
        using handbook appeals
        procedure, 146
    of reference, 23
        ideal, 148
        modest, 147
    as direct evidence of dis-
        crimination, 89
    of thanks or praise, 102

Libel, 83

Lie detector test, 74

Longshoremen's and Harbor
    Workers' Compensation Act
    of 1927, 140

Lump sum payment, 30-31, 48

McDonnell-Douglas Test, 90

Mail fraud, RICO and, 76

Managers, mid-level, 13, 41

Mediation, 121-22

Medical insurance, 75

Memos, internal, 102

Mental disabilities, 70

Merit System Protection Board
    (MSPB), 79-80, 100

Mexican-American Legal De-
    fense and Education Fund,
    142

Mid-level managers, 13, 41

Minimum wage, 80

Misconduct
    discharge for, 40
    gross, 53

Motions to dismiss, 118

MSPB. See Merit System Pro-
    tection Board

NAACP. See National Associa-
    tion for the Advancement of
    Colored People

Name clearing hearing, 58

National Alliance of Senior
    Citizens, 143

National Association for the
    Advancement of Colored
    People (NAACP), 105, 142

National Association of Protec-
    tion and Advocacy systems,
    143

National Association of Work-
    ing Women, 143

National Conference of Black
    Lawyers, 142

National Council of Senior
    Citizens, 143

National Employee Rights
    Institute (NERI), 5, 14, 134,
    143

National Employees Organiza-
    tion (NEO), 5

National Employment Lawyers
    Association (NELA), 105,
    142

National Labor Relations Act
    (NLRA), 66-67, 136

National Labor Relations
    Board (NLRB), 100, 113,
    135, 138-39

National Lawyers Guild, 142

National origin, discrimination
    based on, 67-68, 98, 100,
    110

National Senior Citizens Law
    Center, 143

National Urban League, 142

National Veterans Legal Ser-
    vices Project, 142

Native American Rights Fund,
    142

Negligence, 88

Negotiating
    attorneys' expertise in, 37
    considerations before, 38
    employers' representatives
        for, 38
    strategies for, 38-39
    your own separation pack-
        age, 37-44

NELA. See National Employ-
    ment Lawyers Association

NEO. See National Employees
    Organization

NERI. See National Employee
    Rights Institute

Networking, 124-25

NLRA. See National Labor
    Relations Act

Non-compete clause, 25-26

Non-disparagement agree-
    ment, 41

Non-disparagement clause,
    116

Non-exempt employees, 42

Non-governmental resources,
    142-43

No-show consulting agree-
    ment, 43

Notary Public, 103

Notice period, 43

NOW Legal Defense and Edu-
    cation Fund, 143

Nutrition, 130

Occupational Safety and
    Health Administration
    (OSHA), 100, 135
    complaints to, 114-15
    official citations to, 136
    regional offices, 139-40

Office of Personnel Manage-
    ment, Retirement Opera-
    tions Center, 141

Older Women's League, 143

Older Workers' Benefit Protec-
    tion Act, 24

Oral contracts, 63

Order form, 151

Organization charts, as case
    document, 102

Outplacement services, 43,
    126

Pension Benefit Guaranty Cor-
    poration, 141

Pension Education Clearing-
    house, 143

Pension plan
    discrimination based on
        status in, 94-95
    distribution of, 34
    early retirement and, 42-43
    information about, as case
        document, 102

severance package and, 32
Pension plans
ERISA and, 75
non-governmental resources for information, 143
regulation of, 34
Pension Rights Center, 34, 143
Performance
evaluations, as case document, 102
poor, as termination reason, 16
Perjury, refusal to commit, 87
Personal files, 20
Personnel files
document requests for, 117
request to copy, 21
state laws regarding, 20-21
Piece rate, 80
Plaintiff, 117
Pre-complaint counseling, 112
Pregnancy, discrimination based on, 100, 110
Prejudice, as circumstantial evidence, 89
President's Committee on Employment of People and Disabilities, 142
Prima facie case, 90
Privacy, invasion of, 84-85
Private sector employee, laws protecting, 56-57
Privileged information, 106
Profit-sharing plan
ERISA and, 75
severance package and, 32
Promise
enforceable, 63-64
of job security, 62
Promissory estoppel, 64
as contract claims, 99
state laws for, 99
Protected class, 68, 90-92
Protected conduct, 92-93, 93
Public assistance, 51
Public Law Boards, 76
Public policy
claim, 87
violation of, 99

Puerto Rican Legal Defense and Education Fund, 142
Punitive damages, 120

Qualifications, discrimination on basis of, 90
Qualified privilege, 84
Quitting job. See Resignation

Race
discrimination based on, 67-68, 98, 100, 110
rights of, non-governmental resources for, 142
Racketeer Influenced and Corrupt Organizations Act (RICO), 76, 100, 136
Railroad Retirement Board, 141
Railway Labor Act (RLA), 76, 136
Reasonable accommodation
ADA and, 71
Title VII and, 69
Record of events, 28, 132
Reference letter
effective, 23
negotiating for good, 116
References
for potential employer, 125-26
qualified privilege and, 84
Reinstatement
authority for, 15
as preferred remedy, 120
written request for, 17
Release (of claims), 24-25
attorney to help you understand, 104
deadline for, 39
with large severance package, 30
from possible legal proceeding, 41
Religious discrimination, 69, 98, 100, 110
Remedies, administrative, 110-15
Reprimands, 102

Resignation
due to employer's unlawful conduct, 104
implications of, 21-22, 42
unemployment compensation and, 47
Restrictive covenant, 25-26
Resume, 125
Retainer, 107
Retaliation
claims, 92-94, 110
discrimination based on, 100
Retirement plan, 32-35
early retirement and, 42-43
ERISA and, 75
information about, as case document, 102
severance package and, 32-35
RICO. See Racketeer Influences and Corrupt Organizations Act
Rights
to privacy, 84-85
to sue, 37, 111
understanding your, 13, 104
RLA. See Railway Labor Act
Rules. See Laws

Salary
continuation of, 30-32
discrimination, 79
as termination reason, 16
Sauter, Susan, 3
Savings plan, 32-35
Separation package
considerations for, 30-36
leverage for generous, 22
negotiating your own, 37-44
standard, 41-42
unneeded benefits in, 43-44
See also Severance package; Severance pay
Service letter, 21
Settlement, 24
options, 118

agreements, confidentiality requirements in, 26-27
Severance package
 best possible, 134
 in legitimate downsizing, 38
 in mass layoff, 38
 See also Separation package; Severance pay
Severance pay, 30-32
 attorney negotiating for, 104
 ERISA and, 75
 lump sum payment of, 30-31
 periodic payment of, 31
 salary continuation as, 30-32
 taxability of, 30-31, 44
 unemployment compensation and, 48
Sex
 discrimination based on, 67-68, 98, 100
 non-governmental resources for, 143
 See also Gender
Sexual harassment
 anti-retaliation provisions and, 73
 non-governmental resources for, 143
 RICO and, 76
Sexual orientation, discrimination based on, 98
Sick pay, 32
Sick time, 72
Slander, 83
Social Security Administration, 141
Social Security deduction, 44
Southern Poverty Law Center, 142
SSI. *See* Supplemental Security Income
State laws
 assault and battery, 85-86
 blacklisting, 82
 for contract claims, 99
 defamation, 83-84

discrimination-related, 98-99, 115
false imprisonment, 86-87
fraud, 85
intentional infliction of emotional distress, 83
interference with employment relationship, 88
invasion of privacy, 84-85
negligence, 88
personnel files, 20-21
public policy violation, 87-88
service letter, 21
for tort claims, 99
torts, 82-88
unlawful dismissals, 82
Statutes of limitations, 98-101, 100-01
 federal laws, 98
 nearing end of, 104
 state laws, 98
Stock options, 35-36
Stress, reducing, 130-33
Stress Breakers, 132
Strike, union, 48
Subpoenas, 117
Suitable employment, 49
Summary plan description, 32
Supplemental Security Income (SSI), 70
Support group, 131-32
Support system, 129

Tax
 on pension or savings account withdrawal, 35
 severance pay, 30-31, 44
Telephone calls, employer interference with, 85
Temporary employment agency, 60
Temporary layoffs, 74
Termination
 appealing your, 27
 challenging through grievance process, 16
 deferring effective date of, 43

documentation, 19, 102, 117
education and training after, 128
employers' policies and practices on, 15
for misconduct, 40
no legitimate reason for, 91-92
period of post-, 134
protected conduct and, 93-94
public policy claim for, 87
qualified privilege and, 84
questioning employer about, 13
reason for, 16, 21
redefining the, 42
retirement and savings plans and, 32, 34
unemployment compensation and, 45-46, 50
unjust, state laws prohibiting, 57
unlawful, statutes of limitations for, 100
of "whistleblowing" civil service employee, 59
Threats, 27
Thrift savings plan, 32
Time line, 28
Title VII, 67-69, 71, 95, 100, 111, 136. *See also* Civil Rights Act
Tobias, Paul H., 3
Tort claims, state laws for, 99
Tort of outrage, 83
Torts, 82
Trade secrets, 26-27
Training, after termination, 128
Trial, going to, 119
Tuition reimbursement, 43

U.S. Department of Labor (DOL), 135
 Division of Public Affairs, 142
 as job lead source, 126
 Wage and Hour Division, 100

claims investigated by, 113-14

regional offices, 140-41

Women's Bureau, 143

U.S. Department of Veterans Affairs, 141

U.S. Government Printing Office, 141

U.S. Merit Systems Protections Board. *See* Merit Systems Protections Board

U.S. Postal Service, pre-complaint counseling at, 112

ULP. *See* Unfair labor practices

Undue hardship, religious beliefs and employer's, 69

Unemployment compensation, 45-50

    eligibility for, 45

    information about, as case document, 102

    job postings at office for, 126

    making best of system for, 48-49

    salary continuation and, 31

Unfair labor practices (ULP), 67, 101, 113

Uniformed Services Employment and Reemployment Rights Act of 1994, 76, 100, 136

Union

    arbitration by, 121

    activities claims, 113

    contract violations, 112-13

    grievance procedure of, 57

    not joining, 67

Union employees

    grievance procedures for, 17

    laws protecting, 57-58

    non-governmental resources for, 143

    right to participate in, 66, 100

    unemployment compensation and, 48

United States Code (U.S.C.), 66, 82

United States Office of Special Counsel, 59

Unlawful dismissals, 82

Unsafe working conditions

    claims about, 114-15

    as "good cause" for quitting, 47

    unlawful discharge due to complaints of, 100

Vacation pay, 32

Vacation time, FMLA leave and, 72

Vesting, 33-34, 43, 75

Wages

    discrimination, 79

    employer's financial responsibility for, 36

    garnishment of, 76

    minimum, 80

    unlawful termination and lost, 44

Waiting week, 45

WARN. *See* Worker Adjustment Retraining and Notification Act

Welfare benefit plan

    discrimination based on status in, 94-95

    ERISA and, 75

Welfare system, 51

Whistleblower Protection Act, 78, 136

Whistleblowing

    RICO and, 76

    state laws on, 82

Willful misconduct termination, 46

Wire fraud, RICO and, 76

Witnesses, 28, 103

Women's issues, non-governmental resources for, 143

Women's Legal Defense Fund, 105, 143

Work assignments, 102

Worker Adjustment Retraining and Notification Act (WARN), 73-74, 100-01, 136

Workers compensation claim, 82, 87

Written contracts, 62